D1610565

ROY CAMPBELL
SELECTED POETRY

THE PRINCIPAL WORKS OF ROY CAMPBELL

POETRY

The Flaming Terrapin, Jonathan Cape, 1924
The Wayzgoose, Jonathan Cape, 1928
Adamastor, Faber & Faber, 1930
Gum Trees, Faber & Faber, 1930
The Georgiad, Boriswood, 1931
Pomegranates, Boriswood, 1932
Flowering Reeds, Boriswood, 1933
Mithraic Emblems, Boriswood, 1936
Flowering Rifle, Longmans, 1939
(revised, The Bodley Head, 1957)
Sons of the Mistral, Faber & Faber, 1941
Talking Bronco, Faber & Faber, 1946
Poems of St John of the Cross, Harvill, 1951
Baudelaire's Les Fleurs du Mal, Harvill, 1952
Collected Poems, three volumes, The Bodley Head, 1949-60

PROSE

Broken Record, Boriswood, 1934
Light on a Dark Horse, Hollis & Carter, 1951
Lorca, Bowes & Bowes, 1952
Mamba's Precipice, Frederick Muller, 1953
Portugal, Max Reinhardt, 1957

Roy Campbell

SELECTED POETRY

EDITED BY J. M. LALLEY

THE BODLEY HEAD
LONDON   SYDNEY
TORONTO

ACKNOWLEDGEMENT

The Publishers gratefully acknowledge permission granted
by Messrs Faber & Faber to reprint poems from *Adamastor*
and *Talking Bronco*; by Messrs Jonathan Cape to reprint
The Flaming Terrapin and excerpts from *The Wayzgoose*;
by Messrs Harvill to reprint translations from *The Poems
of St John of the Cross* and from Baudelaire's *Les Fleurs du
Mal*; and by New Directions, New York, representing
the Estate of Federico García Lorca to reprint a number
of poems here translated.

SBN 370 00455 8

Roy Campbell's translation of Horace's The Art of Poetry
© Mary Campbell 1960
Joseph M. Lalley's Foreword and Notes
© The Bodley Head Ltd and Henry Regnery Inc 1968
This edition © Mary Campbell 1968
Printed and bound in Great Britain for
The Bodley Head Ltd
9 Bow Street, London, W C 2
by C. Tinling & Co Ltd, Liverpool, London and Prescot
Set in Monotype Ehrhardt
This edition first published 1968

CONTENTS

EDITOR'S FOREWORD

The present selection, which is intended for the general reader rather than the student, is not chronological. A chronological arrangement would have been in any case difficult, since many of the earlier poems were first published in obscure or inaccessible journals. The aim has been rather to represent the highly varied aspects of the poet's genius —his extremes of tenderness and violence, of sensitivity and sarcasm, his passionate loyalties and animadversions, as well as to illustrate his prosodic versatility and his rare gifts of imagery and metaphor. Some of the long satirical poems are represented only by excerpts, and since this necessarily involves a disruption of continuity I have ventured to insert, here and there, a few thematic sub-titles. The annotations are intended to clarify allusions to persons or incidents that may be unfamiliar to a more recent generation. Occasional notes by the poet himself are marked with his initials.

Much of Roy Campbell's finest work is to be found in his translations from other poets, examples of which occupy the latter pages of this book. Poetical translation is admittedly the most difficult of all literary arts, and many besides Dr Johnson have deemed it an impossible one. Certainly very few translators have succeeded, as Campbell has done, in recreating in an alien idiom not only the form and content but emotional evocations of the originals.

The editor gratefully acknowledges his indebtedness to Mr J. C. van Rooy of the Embassy of South Africa, Washington, for his kind help in clarifying certain details concerning Roy Campbell's association with the magazine *Voorslag*, and in identifying some of the personages mentioned in *The Wayzgoose*.

J. M. L.

LYRICAL
AND
LOVE POEMS

The Making of a Poet

In every herd there is some restive steer
Who leaps the cows and heads each hot stampede,
Till the old bulls unite in jealous fear
To hunt him from the pastures where they feed.

Lost in the night he hears the jungles crash
And desperately, lest his courage fail,
Across his hollow flanks with sounding lash
Scourges the heavy whipcord of his tail.

Far from the phalanxes of horns that ward
The sleeping herds he keeps the wolf at bay,
At nightfall by the slinking leopard spoored,
And goaded by the fly-swarm through the day.

The Festivals of Flight

Too sensitively nerved to bear
Domestication, O my friends
On a perpetual change of air
Whose sole stability depends,

By what phenomenal emotion,
Alas, is each of us obsessed
That travel, flight, and ceaseless motion
Must keep us in a state of rest?

Schooled by the new gymnastic Muse
In barbarous academies,
The rifle and the running noose
Conferred upon us their degrees,

To play our more precarious parts
Trapezed above the rolling decks
Or in the high equestrian arts
To graduate with broken necks.

Yet I could wish, before I perish,
To make my peace with God above
Or, like a millionaire, to cherish
My purse with soft marsupial love,

Or like a poet woo the moon,
Riding an armchair for my steed,
And with a flashing pen harpoon
Terrific metaphors of speed—

Speed, motion, flight!—the last hosanna
Of routed angels: sword that fights
The coward free: unfailing manna
Of earth's fastidious Israelites!

Valise of invalids on tour:
Refuge of refugees in flight:
Home of the homeless: sinecure
Of hunted thieves at dead of night.

Nirvana of the record-breakers,
Heaven in which our senses swim,
Aviary of aviators
And poultry-run of seraphim!

Safari to the unexplored
With rough first-aid for Cupid's darts,
Perambulator of the Bored
And ambulance of broken hearts!

Deranger of the intellects
Of those who flee before a curse,
Fixative of blurred effects,
And laxative of minor verse!

Mecca of all mechanic progress:
Destination, course, and goal
Of those who've none: Circean Ogress
Whose snouted trophy is my soul!

Tourist, who leaves with ten-league boots
His spoor of Castles down the Rhine:
Smoker of immense cheroots—
The funnels of the Cunard Line!

Of cranks, the boomerang and waddy:
Of rogues, the assegai and kerry:
Black Maria to the Body,
To the Soul a Stygian ferry!

Pope of the gypsies: sole religion
Of those who sail with every breeze:
The Son, the Father, and the Pigeon
To wandering aborigines!

To Thee our heathen hymns are hurled
From where we wander in the clouds—
Sonatas on the fog-horn skirled,
The pibroch of the creaking shrouds.

Lead, kindly ignis fatuus, far
Amid the world's encircling gloom:
In my last trek be thou the star
To whom I hitch my disselboom.

Far from the famed memorial arch
Towards a lonely grave I come,
My heart in its funereal march
Goes beating like a muffled drum,[1]

Yet lest when midnight winds are loud
I should not see the way to go,
Let every gross proverbial cloud
Its shabby silver lining show:

And you shall lend me, if you please,
That in the mode I may appear,
Your shirt, tormented Hercules!
Laocoön! your bandolier.

[1] Campbell evidently borrowed this quatrain from his own translation of Baudelaire's *Le Guignon* (Ill Luck) which appears on page 174. The original is

> Loin des sépultures célèbres,
> Vers un cimetière isolé,
> Mon cœur, comme un tambour voilé,
> Va battant des marches funèbres.

The Secret Muse

Between the midnight and the morn,
To share my watches late and lonely,
There dawns a presence such as only
Of perfect silence can be born.
On the blank parchment falls the glow
Of more than daybreak: and one regal
Thought, like the shadow of an eagle,
Grazes the smoothness of its snow.
Though veiled to me that face of faces
And still that form eludes my art,
Yet all the gifts my faith has brought
Along the secret stair of thought
Have come to me on those hushed paces
Whose footfall is my beating heart.

Rounding the Cape

The low sun whitens on the flying squalls,
Against the cliffs the long grey surge is rolled
Where Adamastor from his marble halls
Threatens the sons of Lusus as of old.

Faint on the glare uptowers the dauntless form,
Into whose shade abysmal as we draw,
Down on our decks, from far above the storm,
Grin the stark ridges of his broken jaw.

Across his back, unheeded, we have broken
Whole forests: heedless of the blood we've spilled,
In thunder still his prophecies are spoken,
In silence, by the centuries, fulfilled.

Farewell, terrific shade! though I go free
Still of the powers of darkness art thou Lord:
I watch the phantom sinking in the sea
Of all that I have hated or adored.

The prow glides smoothly on through seas quiescent:
But where the last point sinks into the deep,
The land lies dark beneath the rising crescent,
And Night, the Negro, murmurs in his sleep.

The Zebras

From the dark woods that breathe of fallen showers,
Harnessed with level rays in golden reins,
The zebras draw the dawn across the plains
Wading knee-deep among the scarlet flowers.
The sunlight, zithering their flanks with fire,
Flashes between the shadows as they pass
Barred with electric tremors through the grass
Like wind along the gold strings of a lyre.

Into the flushed air snorting rosy plumes
That smoulder round their feet in drifting fumes,
With dove-like voices call the distant fillies,
While round the herds the stallion wheels his flight,
Engine of beauty volted with delight,
To roll his mare among the trampled lilies.

African Moonrise

The wind with foetid muzzle sniffed its feast,
The carrion town, that lulled its crowds to rest
Like the sprawled carcase of some giant beast
That hives the rustling larvae in its breast.

When the cold moon rose glinting from the fen
And snailed her slime of fire along the hill,
Insomnia, the Muse of angry men,
To other themes had chid my faithless quill.

But wide I flung the shutters on their hinges
And watched the moon as from the gilded mire
Where the black river trails its reedy fringes,
She fished her shadow with a line of fire.

Against her light the dusty palms were charred:
The frogs, her faithless troubadours, were still,
Alone, it seemed, I kept my trusty guard
Over the stone-grey silence of the hill,

Till a starved mongrel tugging at his chain
With fearful jerks, hairless and wide of eye,
From where he crouched, a thrilling spear of pain,
Hurled forth his Alleluia to the sky.

Fierce tremors volted through his bony notches
And shook the skirling bag-pipe of his hide—
Beauty has still one faithful heart who watches,
One last Endymion left to hymn her pride!

Sing on, lone voice! make all the desert ring,
My listening spirit kindles and adores . . .
Such were my voice, had I the heart to sing,
But mine should be a fiercer howl than yours!

To a Pet Cobra

With breath indrawn and every nerve alert,
As at the brink of some profound abyss,
I love on my bare arm, capricious flirt,
To feel the chilly and incisive kiss
Of your lithe tongue that forks its swift caress
Between the folded slumber of your fangs,
And half reveals the nacreous recess
Where death upon those dainty hinges hangs.

Our lonely lives in every chance agreeing,
It is no common friendship that you bring,
It was the desert starved us into being,
The hate of men that sharpened us to sting:
Sired by starvation, suckled by neglect,
Hate was the surly tutor of our youth:
I too can hiss the hair of men erect
Because my lips are venomous with truth.

Where the hard rock is barren, scorched the spring,
Shrivelled the grass, and the hot wind of death
Hornets the crag with whirred metallic wing—
We drew the fatal secret of our breath:
By whirlwinds bugled forth, whose funnelled suction
Scrolls the spun sand into a golden spire,
Our spirits leaped, hosannas of destruction,
Like desert lilies forked with tongues of fire.

Dainty one, deadly one, whose folds are panthered
With stars, my slender Kalihari flower,
Whose lips with fangs are delicately anthered,
Whose coils are volted with electric power,
I love to think how men of my dull nation
Might spurn your sleep with inadvertent heel
To kindle up the lithe retaliation
And caper to the slash of sudden steel.

There is no sea so wide, no waste so steril
But holds a rapture for the sons of strife:
There shines upon the topmost peak of peril
A throne for spirits that abound in life:
There is no joy like theirs who fight alone,
Whom lust or gluttony have never tied,
Who in their purity have built a throne,
And in their solitude a tower of pride.

I wish my life, O suave and silent sphinx,
Might flow like yours in some such strenuous line,
My days the scales, my years the bony links,
The chain the length of its resilient spine:
And when at last the moment comes to strike,
Such venom give my hilted fangs the power,
Like drilling roots the dirty soil that spike,
To sting these rotted wastes into a flower.

The Serf

His naked skin clothed in the torrid mist
That puffs in smoke around the patient hooves,
The ploughman drives, a slow somnambulist,
And through the green his crimson furrow grooves.

His heart, more deeply than he wounds the plain,
Long by the rasping share of insult torn,
Red clod, to which the war-cry once was rain
And tribal spears the fatal sheaves of corn,
Lies fallow now. But as the turf divides
I see in the slow progress of his strides
Over the toppled clods and falling flowers,
The timeless, surly patience of the serf
That moves the nearest to the naked earth
And ploughs down palaces, and thrones, and towers.

The Zulu Girl

When in the sun the hot red acres smoulder,
Down where the sweating gang its labour plies,
A girl flings down her hoe, and from her shoulder
Unslings her child tormented by the flies.

She takes him to a ring of shadow pooled
By thorn-trees: purpled with the blood of ticks,
While her sharp nails, in slow caresses ruled,
Prowl through his hair with sharp electric clicks.

His sleepy mouth plugged by the heavy nipple,
Tugs like a puppy, grunting as he feeds:
Through his frail nerves her own deep languors ripple
Like a broad river sighing through its reeds.

Yet in that drowsy stream his flesh imbibes
An old unquenched unsmotherable heat—
The curbed ferocity of beaten tribes,
The sullen dignity of their defeat.

Her body looms above him like a hill
Within whose shade a village lies at rest,
Or the first cloud so terrible and still
That bears the coming harvest in its breast.

Silence

I know your footfall hushed and frail
Fair siren of the snow-born lake
Whose surface only swans should sail
And only silver hymns should break,
Or thankful prayers devout as this
White trophy of a night of sighs
Where Psyche celebrates the kiss
With which a sister closed her eyes.

From *Flowering Reeds*

I cannot think (so blue the day)
That those fair castalies of dreams
Or the cool naiads of their streams,
Or I, the willow in whose shade
The wandering music was delayed,
Should pass like ghosts away.

The azure triumphs on the height:
Life is sustained with golden arms:
The fire-red cock with loud alarms
Arising, drums his golden wings
And in the victory he sings,
The Sun insults the night.

O flying hair and limbs of fire
Through whose frail forms, that fade and pass,
Tornadoing as flame through grass,
Eternal beauty flares alone
To build herself a blazing throne
Out of the world's desire—

The summer leaves are whirled away:
The fallen chestnut in the grass
Is trampled by the feet that pass
And like the young Madonna's heart
With rosy portals gashed apart
Bleeds for the things I say.

On the Top of the Caderau

The splintering hail of the night was continued
By the shimmering beams of a morning that sinewed
The lowlands with silver, and trawled to the plains,
Rill-threaded, the sweep of its glittering seines:
As we rode to the summit (high over a cliff
It would dizzy the kestrel to plummet) the wind was a stiff
Bee-line to the sun, that it flew like a thundering kite;
Tunny-finned, and humming with gems, in the ocean of light.
And red on the blue-black blinding azure, your coat
Like a banner of fire in the storming of heaven afloat,
A flaunted bridle challenge was swung for the sunbeam to gore
By the jewelled Aquilon, a glittering toreador;
And under the blue-black buffeted rook of your hair
Your face was a silvery cry in the solitude there,
As you reared your white horse on the summit reminding me this—
That the steepest nevadas of rapture rise over the deepest abyss.

Jousé's Horses

Coasting the delta of the dead lagoons,
The patron said 'We're in for dirty weather.
See, here come Jousé's horses, all together,
(Confound the vermin!) making for the dunes.'

And there along the low verge of the land
All silver fire, (Niagara set free!)
A hundred silken streamers swept the sand,
And with them came the wind, and rose the sea!

Autumn

I love to see, when leaves depart,
The clear anatomy arrive,
Winter, the paragon of art,
That kills all forms of life and feeling
Save what is pure and will survive.

Already now the clanging chains
Of geese are harnessed to the moon:
Stripped are the great sun-clouding planes:
And the dark pines, their own revealing,
Let in the needles of the noon.

Strained by the gale the olives whiten
Like hoary wrestlers bent with toil
And, with the vines, their branches lighten
To brim our vats where summer lingers
In the red froth and sun-gold oil.

Soon on our hearth's reviving pyre
Their rotted stems will crumble up:
And like a ruby, panting fire,
The grape will redden on your fingers
Through the lit crystal of the cup.

From *The Golden Shower*

In what wild forms have you explored with me
The myriad labyrinths of earthly lust?
I love to think that as a tall young tree,
Golden with pollen, furred with fiery dust,
I fired my shower of Danae to the gust
Or made a happy pander of the bee:
I love to think that in our primal strength
Two panthers clothed us with a night of stars:
Or, as a stream beneath its nenuphars,
We rippled in the python's flowery length:

23

Or that within the ocean-clearing whale
We sent up rainbows in majestic play,
And that I sought you then, amid a hail
Of crackling pearls and cataracting spray,
As now amid a rain of golden words.

Yet through the dust a myriad times must pass,
In gold of lilies and in green of grass,
Or in the conscious flesh that now is ours,
Our swift protean essence of delight—
Until the earth has burned away in flowers
Until the stars have eaten up the night,
And having strung, like beads upon a thread,
The changing forms in which we now appear
We in that shining revelry shall tread
Of which we act the faint rehearsals here . . .
For when that final rosary is told,
He who is still new-born (though none so old)
The still-unchanging Present, fold from fold
Tearing the veil, will prove to us at last
That there was never Future time nor Past,
But that, a mere illusion in each tense,
Time was the mere reflection of events . . .

*

When all that *was*, or *shall be*, merely *is*,
And all existence is self known in His,
That which we feel today in either sprite,
And that which we know in moments of delight
Will then be fixed. If into you I burn
Or both into that All, or each return
Singly into ourselves—all shall be one,
And in our love some part of this is done,
For though He shines by us, it's not to dim
The least existence that exists in Him.

*

Though we seem merely mortal, what we are,
Is clearly mirrored on a deathless flood.
We change and fade: our dust is strewn afar—
Only the ancient river of our blood,
Rising far-off in unimagined spaces,
Red with the silt and ruin of the past
And churning with the strife of savage races,

Like deep Zambezi goes on rolling past,
Swiftens through us its energies unending,
And reaches out, beneath the shades we cast,
To what vast ocean of the night descending
Or in what sunny lake at last to sleep,
We do not know—save that it turns to foam.
Just here, for us; its currents curl and comb
And all its castalies in thunder leap,
Silvering, forth into a white resilience
Of ecstasy, whose momentary brilliance
And be ourselves no more: for we are fuel
To deathless fires: about us as we play
Eternal forces, hungry for renewal,
Hurtle their live electrons to the fray.

Clouds, crystals, ferns, the ecstasies of matter,
All the fixed forms of beauty, whereunto
Habituated atoms, when they scatter,
By rays and showers are builded up anew—
All these are rhythms woven from the joy
With which live atoms touch, and kiss, and chime,
Yet through the silent chemistry of time,
Weaving smooth harmonies from change and storm,
Come hankering back to their appointed form
As waves to rhythm, or as words to rhyme.

The Sleeper

She lies so still, her only motion
The waves of hair that round her sweep
Revolving to their hushed explosion
Of fragrance on the shores of sleep.
Is it my spirit or her flesh
That takes this breathless silver swoon?
Sleep has no darkness to enmesh
That lonely rival of the moon,
Her beauty, vigilant and white,
That wakeful through the long blue night,
Watches, with my own sleepless eyes,
The darkness silver into day,
And through their sockets burns away
The sorrows that have made them wise.

The Sisters

After hot loveless nights, when cold winds stream
Sprinkling the frost and dew, before the light,
Bored with the foolish things that girls must dream
Because their beds are empty of delight,

Two sisters rise and strip. Out from the night
Their horses run to their low-whistled pleas—
Vast phantom shapes with eyeballs rolling white
That sneeze a fiery steam about their knees:

Through the crisp manes their stealthy prowling hands,
Stronger than curbs, in slow caresses rove,
They gallop down across the milk-white sands
And wade far out into the sleeping cove:

The frost stings sweetly with a burning kiss
As intimate as love, as cold as death:
Their lips, whereon delicious tremors hiss,
Fume with the ghostly pollen of their breath.

Far out on the grey silence of the flood
They watch the dawn in smouldering gyres expand
Beyond them: and the day burns through their blood
Like a white candle through a shuttered hand.

November Nights

On the westmost point of Europe, where it blows with might and main,
While loudly on the village-spires the weathercocks are shrieking,
And gusty showers, like kettledrums, are rattled on the pane,
The rafters like the shrouds of some old sailing-ship are creaking,
And the building reels and rumbles as it rides the wind and rain.

The treetops clash their antlers in their ultimate dishevelry:
The combers crash along the cliffs to swell the dreadful revelry,
And to the nightlong blaring of the lighthouse on the rocks
The fog-horns of the ships reply. The wolves in all their devilry,
Starved out of the sierras, have been slaughtering the flocks.

26

Now peasants shun the muddy fields, and fisherfolk the shores.
It is the time the weather finds the wounds of bygone wars,
And never to a charger did I take as I have done
To cantering the rocking-chair, my Pegasus, indoors,
For my olives have been gathered and my grapes are in the tun.

Between the gusts the wolves raise up a long-drawn howl of woe:
The mastiff whines, with bristled hair, beside us cowering low,
But for the firelight on your face I would not change the sun,
Nor would I change a moment of our winter-season, no,
For our springtime with its orioles and roses long ago.

From *The Rodeo of the Centaurs*

Enormous stallions captain their array
White, colorado, piebald, roan, or grey,
Bearded like rivergods, maned like the lion,
The very firstborn children of Ixion;
With (in their hoofbeats thundering aloud)
The lightnings of their old maternal cloud,
Though in their cries sounds, too, the ring of steel
Which tells of the inexorable wheel,
Around them frisk, and caper, and cavort
The youngsters, fettled out for crazy sport,
Beardless, and bronzed, with pillion-tempting shapes,
Apt for a thousand robberies and rapes
Of nymphs, or lusty dames, or maiden lilies,
Or rustling their own mares and sister-fillies
From their own fathers' care: or waging fights
With satyrs rolling boulders down the heights.
But most of all their mares excite your wonder
In whom the lady cleaves the beast asunder
Forked from the hips into a surge of thunder
Like Venus when half-risen from the breaker,
Waist-deep in foam, she felt the tempest take her;
Amidst the cyclone of her own red hair
Burned motionless in the revolving air;
And in its angry vortex found the calm
Of the still taper and the windless palm.

Or as the sacred aloe skyward rears
That flowers but once in every hundred years
Stirs the dead lava through its crust of snow
Reviving fires that long had ceased to glow,
Resolving these in living sap to run
And rise erupting to the noonday sun,
Till, white without, but red within as blood,
To rift the pod with its explosive bud,
Smoking its pollen forth in fumes of gold
As though the fleece of Colchos were unrolled,
The bloom whose yawn is redder than a panther's,
With a snarl of fire and slash of golden anthers,
Gashes its great glory from the blue—
So from the brute the goddess burgeons through.
Than these two natures, never day and night
At dawn did more magnificently fight;
Nor the pole sheer away from its equator
To such an arctic blaze; nor from its crater
The snow-coned flame more frostily ignite
Its red-gold tresses trawling through the height.

*

Fillies as lovely, stallions thrice as strong
Returned that day to join their tribal throng;
They drank, they danced, they chanted ancient rhymes,
And boasted of the old equestrian times.
Here where, of old, the prince of music makers
Has galloped, rounding up the deep-sea breakers
With music, on a grampus for his steed,
Along the rolling, green, star-covered mead
The Centaurs met once more beside the ocean;
And having praised all life and light and motion,
Earth, Sea and Sky, and their Creator most
Each one returned to his eternal post
And mounted guard in the imagination,
Taking once more his fixed, heraldic station
In poem, sculpture, frieze, or constellation.

*

Hippea there, the boldest of the troop,
Her hand a pistol-shot on her own croup,
Leaping the chasmed stream, romps into sight,
Titupping down the grass with daisies white.

So smoothly to a trot she changed her trippel
That on her breast it scarcely bounced the nipple.
While like a mitrailleuse of silver shots
Her one white stocking flickers as she trots,
She swerved into the forefront of the trek,
Unslung the light guitar from round her neck,
And to its music thrummed herself along:
And there were red carnations in her song
And one, snow-white, behind her ear. Thick shoaled,
Like blood-red mullet in a seine of gold,
The deeper shadows in her chestnut hair.
Freckled like rose-shot apricots, her bare
Shoulders and breasts and neck, beneath whose tan
Blurred veins of jacaranda forked and ran.
She snowed with graces, and her eyes with blue
Electric stars that pitied as they slew.
Like flint to steel her teeth the sunbeams broke
And flashed and sparkled as she smiled or spoke,
Like full red peppers were her laughing lips,
And downward from the snowline of her hips,
Like lava'd slopes, the muscles of the steed
Forth like a mountain torrent hurled her speed
To swirl, to pause, in reveries to doze
Or cataract in thunder as she chose.
The sailing horseflesh like a frigate strong
Followed its matchless figurehead along
And daisies sprang beneath her all the way
To spoor her passage with a wake of spray;
Two thousand years of youth as fair as Flora
Since for this noon she dawned, her own aurora;
When from the breaking cloud and broken Titan
Our breed began to thunder and to lighten,
Stampeding forth on hoofs like rolling boulders,
Or on the red landslide when Vesuvius smoulders—
Out of the womb of ruin leapt her form
And was the rainbow of that raging storm.

*

With the new moon horned in their silver brows,
The waves, like Herefords, came forth to browse
The deep green darkness by the windless shore
Along whose cliffs those hoofs will sound no more.

Canaan

Beneath us stream the golden hours
The slower for our hearts, where now,
Two ripe grenades on the same bough,
Their globes of bronze together swung,
Have stayed the stream they overhung
With fallen heaps of flowers.

For never was she half so fair
Whose colours bleed the red rose white
And milk the lilies of their light:
In her snowed breasts where sorrow dies,
All the white rills of Canaan rise,
And cedars in her hair.

Half-way across a flowery land
Through which our still reluctant feet
Must pass, for every halt too fleet,
We pause upon the topmost hill
Whence streams of wine and honey spill
To some rapacious strand.

There, sisters of the milky way,
The rills of Canaan sing and shine:
Diluvial in the waves of wine
Whose gulls are rosy-footed doves
The glorious bodies of my loves
Like dolphins heave the spray—

Red Rhones towards the sounding shore
Through castled gorges roaring down
By many a tiered and towery town,
High swollen with a spate of hours,
And strewn with all the dying flowers
That we shall love no more—

Torrential in the nightingale,
My spirit hymns them as they go
For wider yet their streams must flow
With flowery trophies heaped more high
Before they drain their sources dry
And those clear fountains fail.

The Dead Torero

From *Mithraic Emblems*

Such work can be the mischief of an hour.
This drunken-looking doll without a face
Was lovely Florentino. This was grace
And virtue smiling on the face of Power.

Shattered, that slim Toledo-tempered spine!
Hollow, the chrysalis, his gentle hand,
From which those wide imperial moths were fanned
Each in its hushed miraculous design!

He was the bee, with danger for his rose!
He died the sudden violence of Kings,
And from the bullring to the Virgin goes
Floating his cape. He has no need for wings.

To the Sun

From *Mithraic Emblems*

Oh let your shining orb grow dim,
Of Christ the mirror and the shield,
That I may gaze through you to Him,
See half the miracle revealed,
And in your seven hues behold
The Blue Man walking on the Sea;
The Green, beneath the summer tree,
Who called the children; then the Gold
With palms; the Orange, flaring bold
With scourges; Purple in the garden
(As Greco saw): and then the Red
Torero (Him who took the toss
And rode the black horns of the cross—
But rose snow-silver from the dead!)

31

Nativity

All creatures then rejoiced, save that the Seven
  Capital steers of whom I am a herder
    (My Cloven heart their hoofprint in the mire)
With bloodshot glare interrogated heaven,
  And, back to back, with lowered horns of murder
    From spiracles of fury spirted fire.

Never so joyfully the brave cocks crew—
  No more by turns, but all with one accord.
  Never so early woke the mule and ox
Since it was day before the east was blue:
  Mary was dawn, the Sunrise was our Lord,
    And Joseph was the watchtower on the rocks.

Never for such a golden quilt lay blooming
  The fields, as for this richly-laden hay,
    And though the frost was sharp before the day,
The mule and ox, whose respiration fuming
  Ignited in the lantern's dim, red ray,
    Warmed him with rosy feathers where he lay.

Far overhead streamed on the signal meteor,
  The Ariadne of the maps, who slowly
    Unwound the light and reeled the darkness up.
Love filled with fierce delight the humblest creature
  As heaven fills an eye, or as the Holy
    Infinitude the wafer and the cup.

Shepherds and kings and cowboys knelt around
  And marvelled that, while they could feel the power
    Whose rapture roars in God, yet God should moan:
And while His glory raised men off the ground
  (For Eve had brought such jewels in her dower)
    The tears of man should shine in God alone.

Washing Day

Amongst the rooftop chimneys where the breezes
Their dizzy choreography design,
Pyjamas, combinations, and chemises
Inflate themselves and dance upon the line.
Drilled by a loose disorder and abandon,
They belly and explode, revolve and swing,
As fearless of the precipice they stand on
As if there were religion in a string.
Annexing with their parachute invasion
The intimate behaviour of our life,
They argue, or embrace with kind persuasion,
And parody our dalliance or our strife.
We change ideas and moods like shirts or singlets,
Which, having shed, they rise to mock us still:
And the wind laughs and shakes her golden ringlets
To set them independent of our will.
They curtsey and collapse, revolve and billow—
A warning that, when least aware we lie,
The dreams are incubated in our pillow
That animate its chrysalis to fly.

San Juan de la Cruz

When that brown bird, whose fusillading heart
Is triggered on a thorn the dark night through,
Has slain the only rival of his art
That burns, with flames for feathers, in the blue—
I think of him in whom those rivals met
To burn and sing, both bird and star, in one:
The planet slain, the nightingale would set
To leave a pyre of roses for the Sun.
His voice an iris through its rain of jewels—
Or are they tears, those embers of desire,
Whose molten brands each gust of song re-fuels?—
He crucifies his heart upon his lyre,
Phoenix of Song, whose deaths are his renewals,
With pollen for his cinders, bleeding fire!

Canidia and Priapus

(Adapted from Horace's Satire)

When old Canidia ghosted on the prowl
To serenade you with her grisly choir,
Whose trombone is the toad, whose flute the owl,
And jingled wealth her soul—destructive lyre:
Presenting arms, the sentry of the garden,
With resolute backfire, I dinned the night,
Whose thunder served our slack morale to harden,
Reversing all the gears of her delight.
That thunder was the sacred power of verse
That bowed her towering Castle with its curse
And to the peering rabble gave the keep:
While with such ridicule it struck her charms
The nymphs ran screaming from her outstretched arms
While she retired in Solitude to weep.

Luiz de Camões

Camões, alone, of all the lyric race,
Born in the angry morning of disaster,
Can look a common soldier in the face:
I find a comrade where I sought a master:
For daily, while the stinking crocodiles
Glide from the mangroves on the swampy shore,
He shares my awning on the dhow, he smiles,
And tells me that he lived it all before.
Through fire and shipwreck, pestilence and loss,
Led by the ignis fatuus of duty
To a dog's death—yet of his sorrows king—
He shouldered high his voluntary Cross,
Wrestled his hardships into forms of beauty,
And taught his gorgon destinies to sing.

Juba River, 1944

34

Interval
From *Kwa Heri*!

Like endless flocks of orient fleeces
Chiming with birds instead of bells
The lit mimosas from their branches
Let fall the spicy avalanches
Which every waking breeze releases,
Or bird, that in their frondage dwells.

Drive forth your hopes like steers and heifers
To graze across these golden plains
Since now for one freak hour is focused
No threat of hailstorm, drought or locust,
And now the gentlest of the zephyrs
Leads home the lions by their manes.

NARRATIVE
AND
ALLEGORICAL POEMS

Hialmar

The firing ceased and like a wounded foe
The day bled out in crimson: wild and high
A far hyena sent his voice of woe
Tingling in faint hysteria through the sky.

Thick lay the fatal harvest of the fight
In the grey twilight when the newly-dead
Collect those brindled scavengers of night
Whose bloodshot eyes must candle them to bed.

The dead slept on: but one among them rose
Out of his trance, and turned a patient eye
To where like cankers in a burning rose,
Out of the fading scarlet of the sky,

Great birds, descending, settled on the stones:
He knew their errand and he knew how soon
The wolf must make a pulpit of his bones
To skirl his shrill hosannas to the moon.

Great adjutants came wheeling from the hills,
And chaplain crows with smug, self-righteous face,
And vultures bald and red about the gills
As any hearty colonel at the base.

All creatures that grow fat on beauty's wreck,
They ranged themselves expectant round the kill,
And like a shrivelled arm each raw, red neck
Lifted the rusty dagger of its bill.

Then to the largest of that bony tribe
'O merry bird', he shouted, 'work your will,
I offer my clean body as a bribe
That when upon its flesh you've gorged your fill,

'You'll take my heart and bear it in your beak
To where my sweetheart combs her yellow hair
Beside the Vaal: and if she bids you speak
Tell her you come to represent me there.

'Flounce out your feathers in their sleekest trim,
Affect the brooding softness of the dove—
Yea, smile, thou skeleton so foul and grim,
As fits the bland ambassador of love!

'And tell her, when the nights are wearing late
And the grey moonlight smoulders on her hair,
To brood no more upon her ghostly mate
Nor on the phantom children she would bear.

'Tell her I fought as blindly as the rest,
That none of them had wronged me whom I killed,
And she may seek within some other breast
The promise that I leave her unfulfilled.

'I should have been too tired for love or mirth
Stung as I am, and sickened by the truth—
Old men have hunted beauty from the earth
Over the broken bodies of our youth!'

Tristan da Cunha

Snore in the foam; the night is vast and blind;
The blanket of the mist about your shoulders,
Sleep your old sleep of rock, snore in the wind,
Snore in the spray! the storm your slumber lulls,
His wings are folded on your nest of boulders
As on their eggs the grey wings of your gulls.

No more as when, so dark an age ago,
You hissed a giant cinder from the ocean,
Around your rocks you furl the shawling snow
Half sunk in your own darkness, vast and grim,
And round you on the deep with surly motion
Pivot your league-long shadow as you swim.

Why should you haunt me thus but that I know
My surly heart is in your own displayed,
Round whom such leagues in endless circuit flow,
Whose hours in such a gloomy compass run—
A dial with its league-long arm of shade
Slowly revolving to the moon and sun.

My pride has sunk, like your grey fissured crags,
By its own strength o'ertoppled and betrayed:
I, too, have burned the wind with fiery flags
Who now am but a roost for empty words,
An island of the sea whose only trade
Is in the voyages of its wandering birds.

Did you not, when your strength became your pyre,
Deposed and tumbled from your flaming tower,
Awake in gloom from whence you sank in fire,
To find, Antaeus-like, more vastly grown,
A throne in your own darkness, and a power
Sheathed in the very coldness of your stone?

Your strength is that you have no hope or fear,
You march before the world without a crown,
The nations call you back, you do not hear,
The cities of the earth grow grey behind you,
You will be there when their great flames go down
And still the morning in the van will find you.

You march before the continents, you scout
In front of all the earth; alone you scale
The mast-head of the world, a lorn look-out,
Waving the snowy flutter of your spray
And gazing back in infinite farewell
To suns that sink and shores that fade away.

From your grey tower what long regrets you fling
To where, along the low horizon burning,
The great swan-breasted seraphs soar and sing,
And suns go down, and trailing splendours dwindle,
And sails on lonely errands unreturning
Glow with a gold no sunrise can rekindle.

Turn to the night; these flames are not for you
Whose steeple for the thunder swings its bells;
Grey Memnon, to the tempest only true,
Turn to the night, turn to the shadowing foam,
And let your voice, the saddest of farewells,
With sullen curfew toll the grey wings home.

41

The wind, your mournful syren, haunts the gloom;
The rocks, spray-clouded, are your signal guns
Whose stony nitre, puffed with flying spume,
Rolls forth in grim salute your broadside hollow
Over the gorgeous burials of suns
To sound the tocsin of the storms that follow.

Plunge forward like a ship to battle hurled,
Slip the long cables of the failing light,
The level rays that moor you to the world:
Sheathed in your armour of eternal frost,
Plunge forward, in the thunder of the fight
To lose yourself as I would fain be lost.

Exiled like you and severed from my race
By the cold ocean of my own disdain,
Do I not freeze in such a wintry space,
Do I not travel through a storm as vast
And rise at times, victorious from the main,
To fly the sunrise at my shattered mast?

Your path is but a desert where you reap
Only the bitter knowledge of your soul:
You fish with nets of seaweed in the deep
As fruitlessly as I with nets of rhyme—
Yet forth you stride, yourself the way, the goal,
The surges are your strides, your path is time.

Hurled by what aim to what tremendous range!
A missile from the great sling of the past,
Your passage leaves its track of death and change
And ruin on the world: you fly beyond
Leaping the current of the ages vast
As lightly as a pebble skims a pond.

The years are undulations in your flight
Whose awful motion we can only guess—
Too swift for sense, too terrible for sight,
We only know how fast behind you darken
Our days like lonely beacons of distress:
We know that you stride on and will not harken.

Now in the eastern sky the fairest planet
Pierces the dying wave with dangled spear,
And in the whirring hollows of your granite
That vaster sea to which you are a shell
Sighs with a ghostly rumour, like the drear
Moan of the nightwind in a hollow cell.

We shall not meet again; over the wave
Our ways divide, and yours is straight and endless,
But mine is short and crooked to the grave:
Yet what of these dark crowds amid whose flow
I battle like a rock, aloof and friendless,
Are not their generations vague and endless
The waves, the strides, the feet on which I go?

In Memoriam of Mosquito, my partner in the horse-trade, gipsy of the Lozoya Clan[1]

I never felt such glory
As handcuffs on my wrists.
My body stunned and gory
With toothmarks on my fists:
The triumph through the square,
My horse behind me led,
A pistol at my cutlets
Three rifles at my head:
And four of those Red bastards
To hold one wounded man
To all the staring rabble
Proclaiming thus my clan.
Then in the high grey prison
They threw me on the straw,

[1] One day I told Mosquito he could go home, as I was invited to have a drink
with the farmer near Buena Vista on the Talavera Road. I had the drink, heard some
firing and rode on to catch up with Mosquito. I found him lying dead by the side
of the bare field near the horse trough that you can see in the foreground of Greco's
painting of Toledo. He held his unopened knife in his hand and there were three
bullet wounds in his body. The tracks of Gaona had swerved off the road on the
bare turf ... Apparently [the Red assault guards] had just been trying out their
new arms and having a bit of sport practice. . . *Light on a Dark Horse*, pp. 306-7.

And through the grille beside me,
Beyond the bridge, I saw
Our other horse 'Gaona',
Across the sand-hills fled
With empty saddle: then I knew,
'Mosquito', you were dead,
And low on the meseta
The sun was turning red.
Across the desert sand-hills
It slowly bled from sight,
And like a horse, a huge black wind
Fled screaming through the night.

Mazeppa[1]

Helpless, condemned, yet still for mercy croaking
Like a trussed rooster swinging by the claws,
They hoisted him: they racked his joints asunder;
They lashed his belly to a thing of thunder—
A tameless brute, with hate and terror smoking,
That never felt the bit between its jaws.

So when his last vain struggle had subsided,
His gleeful butchers wearied of the fun:
Looping the knots about his thighs and back,
With lewd guffaws they heard his sinews crack,
And laughed to see his lips with foam divided,
His eyes too glazed with blood to know the sun.

[1] Ivan Stepanovich Mazepa, or Mazeppa (c. 1640–1709) was reared as a page at
the court of John Casimir, King of Poland, until he was discovered in an amorous
intrigue with a lady of high nobility. The outraged husband ordered that he be
stripped naked and tied to the back of a wild horse. After a cruel beating the horse
was turned loose and set off at a mad gallop over steppes and through forests and
across streams until it reached a cossack village on the lower Dnieper where Mazepa
was released and nursed back to health by the inhabitants. He became a leader
among the cossacks, and with the aid of the then powerful Prince Vasili Golitsyn
was made hetman of the Ukraine. Later he was one of the most trusted generals of
Peter the Great, but secretly conspired against him with Charles XII of Sweden,
with whom he ultimately joined forces. After the disaster at Poltava, Mazepa fled
with the remnant of his horsemen to Turkey where he died. Mazepa's agony on the
back of the wild horse is also the theme of a well-known poem by Lord Byron.

A whip cracked, they were gone: alone they followed
The endless plain: the long day volleyed past
With only the white clouds above them speeding
And the grey steppe into itself receding,
Where each horizon, by a vaster swallowed,
Repeated but the bareness of the last.

Out of his trance he wakened: on they flew:
The blood ran thumping down into his brain:
With skull a-dangle, facing to the sky
That like a great black wind went howling by,
Foaming, he strove to gnash the tethers through
That screwed his flesh into a knot of pain.

To him the earth and sky were drunken things—
Bucked from his senses, jolted to and fro,
He only saw them reeling hugely past,
As sees a sailor soaring at the mast,
Who retches as his sickening orbit swings
The sea above him and the sky below.

Into his swelling veins and open scars
The python cords bit deeper than before
And the great beast, to feel their sharpened sting,
Looping his body in a thundrous sling
As if to jolt his burden to the stars,
Recoiled, and reared, and plunged ahead once more.

Three days had passed, yet could not check nor tire
That cyclone whirling in its spire of sand:
Charged with resounding cordite, as they broke
In sudden flashes through the flying smoke,
The fusillading hoofs in rapid fire
Rumbled a dreary volley through the land.

Now the dark sky with gathering ravens hums:
And vultures, swooping down on his despair,
Struck at the loose and lolling head whereunder
The flying coffin sped, the hearse of thunder,
Whose hoof-beats with the roll of muffled drums
Led on the black processions of the air.

The fourth sun saw the great black wings descending
Where crashed in blood and spume the charger lay:
From the snapped cords a shapeless bundle falls—
Scarce human now, like a cut worm he crawls
Still with a shattered arm his face defending
As inch by inch he drags himself away.

Who'd give a penny for that strip of leather?
Go, set him flapping in a field of wheat,
Or take him as a pull-through for your gun,
Or hang him up to kipper in the sun,
Or leave him here, a strop to hone the weather
And whet the edges of the wind and sleet.

Who on that brow foresees the gems aglow?
Who, in that shrivelled hand, the sword that swings
Wide as a moonbeam through the farthest regions,
To crop the blood-red harvest of the legions,
Making amends to every cheated crow
And feasting vultures on the fat of kings.

This is that Tartar prince, superbly pearled,
Whose glory soon on every wind shall fly,
Whose arm shall wheel the nations into battle,
Whose warcry, rounding up the tribes like cattle,
Shall hurl his cossacks rumbling through the world
As thunder hurls the hail-storm through the sky.

And so it is whenever some new god,
Boastful, and young, and avid of renown,
Would make his presence known upon the earth—
Choosing some wretch from those of mortal birth,
He takes his body like a helpless clod
And on the croup of genius straps it down.

With unseen hand he knots the cord of pain,
Unseen the wingèd courser strains for flight:
He leads it forth into some peopled space
Where the dull eyes of those who throng the place
See not the wings that wave, the thews that strain,
But only mark the victim of their might.

Left for the passing rabble to admire,
He fights for breath, he chokes, and rolls his eyes:
They mime his agonies with loud guffaws,
They pelt him from the place with muddy paws,
Nor do they hear the sudden snort of fire
To which the tether snaps, the great wings rise . . .

Vertiginously through the heavens rearing,
Plunging through chasms of eternal pain,
Splendours and horrors open on his view,
And wingèd fiends like fiercer kites pursue,
With hateful patience at his side careering,
To hook their claws of iron on his brain.

With their green eyes his solitude is starlit,
That lamp the dark and lurk in every brier:
He sinks obscure into the night of sorrow
To rise again, refulgent on the morrow,
With eagles for his ensigns, and the scarlet
Horizon for his Rubicon of fire.

Out of his pain, perhaps, some god-like thing,
Is born. A god has touched him, though with whips:
We only know that, hooted from our walls,
He hurtles on his way, he reels, he falls,
And staggers up to find himself a king
With truth a silver trumpet at his lips.

The Fight[1]

One silver-white and one of scarlet hue,
Storm-hornets humming in the wind of death,
Two aeroplanes were fighting in the blue
Above our town; and if I held my breath,
It was because my youth was in the Red
While in the White an unknown pilot flew—
And that the White had risen overhead.

[1] The aerial combat here described seems to allegorize the spiritual conflict and crisis which preceded the poet's conversion. However, in a preface to a revised version of *The Flowering Rifle*, he described the poem, written in 1935, as a prophetic vision of the Civil War and of its outcome.

From time to time the crackle of a gun
Far into flawless ether faintly railed,
And now, mosquito-thin, into the Sun,
And now like mating dragonflies they sailed:
And, when like eagles near the earth they drove,
The Red, still losing what the White had won,
The harder for each lost advantage strove.

So lovely lay the land—the towers and trees
Taking the seaward counsel of the stream:
The city seemed, above the far-off seas,
The crest and turret of a Jacob's dream,
And those two gun-birds in their frantic spire
At death-grips for its ultimate regime—
Less to be whirled by anger than desire.

Till (Glory!) from his chrysalis of steel
The Red flung wide the fatal fans of fire:
I saw the long flames, ribboning, unreel,
And slow bitumen trawling from his pyre.
I knew the ecstasy, the fearful throes,
And the white phoenix from his scarlet sire,
As silver in the Solitude he rose.

The towers and trees were lifted hymns of praise,
The city was a prayer, the land a nun:
The noonday azure strumming all its rays
Sang that a famous battle had been won,
As signing his white Cross, the very Sun,
The Solar Christ and captain of my days
Zoomed to the zenith; and his will was done.

The Skull in the Desert

I am not one his bread who peppers
With stars of nebulous illusion,
But learned, with soldiers, mules, and lepers
As comrades of my education,
The Economy of desolation
And Architecture of confusion

On the bare sands, where nothing else is
Save death, and like a lark in love,
Gyrating through the vault above,
The ace of all created things
Flies singing Gloria in Excelsis
And spreads the daybreak from his wings:

I found a horse's empty cranium,
Which the hyenas had despised,
Wherein the wind ventriloquized
And fluting huskily afar
Sang of the rose and the geranium
And evenings lit with azahar.

Foaled by the Apocalypse, and stranded
Some wars, or plagues, or famines back,
To bleach beside the desert track,
He kept his hospitable rule:
A pillow for the roving bandit,
A signpost to the stricken mule.

A willing host, adeptly able,
Smoking a long cheroot of flame,
To catalyse the sniper's aim
Or entertain the poet's dream,
By turns a gunrest or a table,
An inspiration, and a theme—

He served the desert for a Sphinx
And to the wind for a guitar,
For in the harmony he drinks
To rinse his whirring casque of bone
There hums a rhythm less its own
Than of the planet and the star.

No lion with a lady's face
Could better have become the spot
Interrogating time and space
And making light of their replies
As he endured the soldier's lot
Of dissolution, sand, and flies.

So white a cenotaph to show
You did not have to be a banker
Or poet of the breed we know:
Subjected to a sterner law,
The luckless laughter of the ranker
Was sharked upon his lipless jaw.

All round, the snarled and windrowed sands
Expressed the scandal of the waves,
And in this orphan of the graves
As in a conch, there seemed to roar
Reverberations of the Hand
That piles the wrecks along the shore.

Twice I had been the Ocean's refuse
As now the flotsam of the sand
Far worse at sea upon the land
Than ever in the drink before
For Triton, with his sons and nephews,
To gargle and to puke ashore.

To look on him, my tongue could taste
The bony mandibles of death
Between my cheeks: across the waste
The drought was glaring like a gorgon
But in that quaint outlandish organ
With spectral whinny, whirled the breath.

The wind arrived, the gorgon-slayer,
Defied the dust that rose to whelm it,
And swirled like water in the helmet
Of that dead brain, with crystal voices,
Articulating in a prayer
The love with which the rain rejoices—

The Zephyr from the blue Nevadas,
Stirrupped with kestrels, smoothly rinking
The level wave where halcyons drowse,
Came with the whirr of the cicadas,
With the green song of orchards drinking
And orioles fluting in the boughs.

All the green juices of creation,
And those with which our veins are red,
Were mingled in his jubilation

And sang the swansong of the planet
Amidst the solitudes of granite
And the grey sands that swathe the dead.

All I had left of will or mind,
Which fire or fever had not charred,
Was but the shaving, husk, and shard:
But that sufficed to catch the air
And from the pentecostal wind
Conceive the whisper of a prayer.

And soon that prayer became a hymn
By feeding on itself. The skies
Were tracered by the seraphim
With arrows from the dim guitars
That on their strings funambulize
The tap-dance of the morning stars.

When frowsy proverbs lose their force
And tears have dried their queasy springs,
To hope and pray for crowns and wings
It follows as a thing of course,
When you've phrenologized the horse
That on the desert laughs and sings.

I leave the Helmet and the Spear
To the hyena-bellied muses
That farm this carnage from the rear:
But of the sacrifice they fear
And of the strain their sloth refuses
Elect me as the engineer.

Make of my bones your fife and organ,
Red winds of pestilence and fire!
But from the rust on the barbed-wire
And scurf upon the pool that stinks
I fetch a nosegay for the Gorgon
And a conundrum for the Sphinx.

For all the freight of Stygian ferries,
Roll on the days of halcyon weather,
The oriole fluting in the cherries,
The sunlight sleeping on the farms,
To say the Rosary together
And sleep in one another's arms!

After the Horse-fair

A mule, the snowball of a beast!
(Ring out the duros, test the tune)
And a guitar, the midnight lark,
That rises silvering the dark
An hour before the rosy-fleeced
Arrival of the Moon.

The gypsies quarried from the gloom,
For their carouse, a silver hall:
And jingled harness filled the lands
With gay pesetas changing hands,
So silvery, there seemed no room
For any moon at all.

Two figtrees on a whitewashed wall
Were playing chess; a lamp was queen:
Beneath the civil guard were seen
With tricorned hats—a game of cards:
One bottle was between them all,
Good health, and kind regards.

A stable with an open door
And in the yard a dying hound:
Out on the dunes a broken spoor
Converging into twenty more—
When torches had been flashed around
Was all they could restore.

A wind that blows from other countries
Shook opals from the vernal palms
Birdshot of the silver huntress
By which the nightingale was slain:
With stitch of fire the distant farms
Were threaded by the train.

One rider, then, and all alone—
The long Castilian Veld before:
To show the way his shadow straight
Went on ahead and would not wait,
But seemed, so infinitely grown,
Equator to the moor.

Till with a faint adoring thunder,
Their lances raised to Christ the King,
Through all the leagues he had to go—
An army chanting smooth and low,
Across the long mirage of wonder
He heard the steeples sing.

And as, far off, the breaking morn
Had hit the high seraphic town,
He prayed for lonesome carbineers
And wakeful lovers, rash of years,
Who've harvested the lunar corn
Before the crops were brown.

For thieves: the gate-man late and lonely
With his green flag; for tramps that sprawl:
And lastly for a frozen guy
That towed six mules along the sky
And felt among them all the only,
Or most a mule of all!

Ballad of Don Juan Tenorio and the Statue
of the Comendador

Ten cuckolds, slain without confession
In duels, by the waterfront
Of Hades, in a glum procession
Are singing out for Charon's punt.

Ten weeping women dry their clothes
Washed up along the homeless sands
By the red sea of perjured oaths
That shoals with amputated hands.

These were the fruits of all your swagger!
But through their tears will swim no more
Those ice-cold fish, your sword and dagger,
Whose fin-wake is a streak of gore;

For now the hour is aiming at you,
Tenorio! with its finger hooked:
Remember when you cuffed the statue
Upon the grave: and how it looked:

And how it seemed to nod its head
When you invited it to dine.
If you were wise to tempt the dead
You verify tonight, at nine.

The stars are like cicadas chirping
With cold: but it is snug in here,
The throne of opulence usurping,
Beneath this costly chandelier.

The firelight twinkles on the jewels
Of pistol-butts: the rays enthrall
The glinting cutlery of duels
That hang for trophies round the wall.

Your Rolls sleeps safely in its garage,
Your Derby-winner in his stall:
But with a prayer balloon your barrage
Against the doom that's due to fall.

Pay off your cook and sack your butler:
Renounce your sacrilegious vow:
Though Satan were Toledo's cutler
No swordplay could avail you now.

A sentence Lawyers cannot garble
Has just been read: the tombs are still:
But from their garrisons of marble
One headstone moves along the hill.

The wind begins to grow much colder,
The grass with icicles to clink:
To pedestal the skating boulder
Each rivulet becomes a rink.

The river bridged itself with crystal
To its refrigerating tread.
The moon rose masked, and cocked the pistol
Of silence to the world's bald head.

Its passing starched the breath of bulls
Along the Guadalquivir's shore.
And froze the ferryman who pulls
More at his wineskin than his oar.

It seems your hounds have scented trouble.
The room grows arctic: moments drag:
Tenorio! pour yourself a double
To entertain the stalking crag.

Tenorio! it's too late for banter,
The statue knocks; the door gives way:
The whisky froze in the decanter
And has not melted to this day.

One handshake: then the detonation
A stench of nitre fills the hall:
The butler on investigation
Retrieved one tiepin: that was all.

Out to the tombs the Civil Guard
Followed the clues of all they heard.
But though one hand seemed slightly charred,
The statue would not speak one word.

One Transport Lost

Where, packed as tight as space can fit them
The soldiers retch, and snore, and stink,
It was no bunch of flowers that hit them
And woke them up, that night, to drink.

Dashing the bulkheads red with slaughter,
In the steep wash that swept the hold,
Men, corpses, kitbags, blood, and water,
Colliding and commingling rolled.

Some clung, like flies, in fear and wonder,
Clutched to the crossbeams, out of reach,
Till sprayed from thence by jets of thunder
That spouted rumbling from the breach.

55

In this new world of blast and suction,
The bulk-head tilted to a roof;
Friend aided friend—but to destruction,
And valour seemed its own reproof.

Forced by the pent explosive airs
In the huge death-gasp of its shell,
Or sucked, like Jonah, by their prayers
From forth that spiracle of Hell—

The ones that catapulted from it
Saw the whole hull reverse its dome,
Then ram the depths, like some huge comet,
Flood-lit with phosphorus and foam.

The shark and grampus might reprieve,
After their jaunt upon a raft,
The few that got Survivor's Leave—
But those who perished would have laughed!

Their fiercest thirst they've quenched and cupped,
And smashed the glass (this life of slaves!);
No hectoring Redcaps interrupt
Their fornication with the waves.

For us, this world of Joad and Julian,
The dithering of abortive schemes;
For them, the infinite, cerulean
Suspension of desires and dreams.

So save your Bait, you Bards and Thinkers!
For us who daren't refuse to chew
Hook, line, and swivel, trace and sinkers,
And rod and all, and like it too!

For them, the wave, the melancholy
Chant of the wind that tells no lies;
The breakers roll their funeral volley
To which the thundering cliff replies.

The black cape-hens in decent crêpe
Will mourn them till the Last Event;
The roaring headlands of the Cape
Are lions on their monument.

Cape Town, 1940

From *The Moon of Short Rations*

Sound me the clash of eating-irons—
The wars where grease and gravy mix!
For in the wind I hear the sirens
Of convoys steaming up the Styx,
And here the rising moon enamels
The skulls of donkeys, mules, and camels,
Whose bonework trellises the track
From here to Headquarters and back,
Which vultures indicate by day
Who roost upon the cook-house shack
Too listless to be scared away.

*

Sing me of Sleeping-car safaris
Through townships blown to smithereens:
The Gold-rush to the Manzanares
Of Bishops, Bards, and Picture-queens
With limelight free, and central heating,
Speeches, and healths, and fat men eating,
While children fought for stale sardines
The better to enhance their pity
And appetize the cocktail snack.
And in the sewers of the city
We groped, and fought, and stumbled back.
Rivers of burgundy were roaring,
Burgundy that was blood of lives—
Poets, at Circe's shrine adoring,
Sound me the clash of forks and knives!

*

In better lands the green leaves mottle,
And Boreas opens out his throttle
Down speedways chevroned by the storks.
Lit by the red lamp of the bottle,
Flashes the play of knives and forks.
The Autumn comes with blare of snails
By shepherds blown with lungs of leather,
And where each huddled foothill quails
Beneath huge thundergrapes of weather,
The flocks descend to stockyard rails.

57

Great hides are stretching in the tannery,
The fat wind reeks with roasted beasts:
Gold in the twilight of the granary
Shimmer the nebulae of feasts.
And out of doors, behold, at morn,
The Samson tresses of the corn—
The strength of armies that expands,
And, vast as ocean, seems to spread
A blond Sahara, sown with hands,
Whose waves are blood, whose sands are bread.
There, when September winds were strident,
Amidst the sword-clash of the reeds,
We flew the sunrise on our trident
Above the groundswell of our steeds
That thundered into suds of spray,
Like some of those that Neptune breeds,
To race them, on the windy bay.
To the guitar that thrilled and bounded,
With female torso on one's thigh—
Valhallan healths and songs resounded,
Till morning, when the tun ran dry.

                              *

But now—the vigil with the slain!
Now is the Ramadan of lions,
When he who fought for Christ in Spain
Atoning, to remove the blot,
Crusades for Woolworths and for Lyons,
Tom Driberg, and the ghostly train
Whose love will wash away the spot.
Like shells with which the beach is starry,
Chalking their whiteness down the shore,
I watch the motionless safari
Of transport that will trek no more,
The caravan of bones, that reaches
To fetch the moon through craggy breaches
Along the avenue of dunes,
With sorrow for the white askari
And hunger for his black platoons.
The ether hums with strange reports,
The winds are dithering wild with news:
Through Africa, huge reefs of quartz
Grind, like the gilded teeth of Jews;

The east is conquering the west;
The future has a face to flee;
The vultures on the cookhouse nest
Like Poets on the B.B.C.

*

Rocked by the fever in his bunk
The flyblown conscript sees with dread
From his decapitated trunk
The moon remove his rolling head
(Salome whom the fiends predestine!)
And wrap it in the picture-paper,
And place it in her silver messtin,
And up the range revolve and caper
A fox-trot which the winds pursue—
He wakes up howling for his mother
Bathed in a cold mercurial dew.
The strandwolfs call to one another:
Surely some rations must be due!
Give me deep dreams, and may I waken
To the artillery of corks:
And down the mountain sides of bacon,
From thunderclouds of steam, be shaken
Lightnings of cutlery and forks!

Eritrea

THE
FLAMING TERRAPIN

THE FLAMING TERRAPIN

This prodigious work was accomplished during the two years the young poet and his wife spent in a remote and primitive Welsh fishing village soon after their marriage in 1922. When it was published in 1924 it immediately established Campbell as a writer of extraordinary imaginative powers and prosodic virtuosity. The poem with its violent and exuberant imagery was in startling contrast to the anaemic style of verse then prevalent. The novelist Arnold Bennett found himself fascinated by the 'emotions, crude and primeval', that surged out of the poet 'in terrific waves'. The famous Irish poet and essayist 'AE' (George Russell) said he knew of no one else who could command 'such a savage splendour of epithet or could marry the wild word so fittingly to the wild thought.' Others began to speak of a new and more tempestuous Byron. The enthusiasm, however, was not quite universal; some thought the poem too rhetorical and bombastic, and Miss Harriet Monroe was later to complain scornfully of Campbell's 'adolescent posturing'.

The Flaming Terrapin (here republished in full) appears to combine some Bantu creation myth with the biblical story of Noah and the flood. The indefatigable Terrapin—he has no resemblance whatever to the familiar diamond-back terrapin of our Atlantic tidewaters—seems to symbolize the human spirit, by turns destructive and creative, self-defeating and self-redeeming. The critics are probably right who have detected in many of Campbell's ebullient images the influence of the French decadents, especially Rimbaud.

The reader will observe how the alternately rhymed pentameter lines suddenly give way to shorter or longer passages in Campbell's favourite narrative vehicle, the heroic couplet, and are as suddenly resumed. In Part Five, coincident with the change of mood, the general iambic pattern is abandoned for passages in varying meters but is restored in the concluding section.

PART ONE

Maternal Earth stirs redly from beneath
Her blue sea-blanket and her quilt of sky,
A giant Anadyomene from the sheath
And chrysalis of darkness; till we spy

Her vast barbaric haunches, furred with trees,
Stretched on the continents, and see her hair
Combed in a surf of fire along the breeze
To curl about the dim sierras, where
Faint snow-peaks catch the sun's far-swivelled beams:
And, tinder to his rays, the mountain-streams
Kindle, and volleying with a thunder-stroke
Out of their roaring gullies, burst in smoke
To shred themselves as fine as women's hair,
And hoop gay rainbows on the sunlit air.
Winnowed by radiant eagles, in whose quills
Sing the swift gales, and on whose waving plumes
Flashing sunbeams ignite—the towering hills
Yearn to the sun, rending the misty fumes
That clogged their peaks, and from each glistening spire
Fling to the winds their rosy fleece of fire.
Far out to sea the gales with savage sweep
Churning the water, waken drowsy fins
Huge fishes to propel from monstrous sleep,
That spout their pride as the red day begins,
'We are the great volcanoes of the deep!'

Now up from the intense creative Earth
Spring her strong sons: the thunder of their mirth
Vibrates upon the shining rocks and spills
In floods of rolling music on the hills.
Action and flesh cohere in one clean fusion
Of force with form: the very ethers breed
Wild harmonies of song: the frailest reed
Holds shackled thunder in its heart's seclusion.
And every stone that lines my lonely way,
Sad tongueless nightingale without a wing,
Seems on the point of rising up to sing
And donning scarlet for its dusty grey!
How often have I lost this fervent mood,
And gone down dingy thoroughfares to brood
On evils like my own from day to day;
'Life is a dusty corridor,' I say,
'Shut at both ends.' But far across the plain,
Old Ocean growls and tosses his grey mane,
Pawing the rocks in all his old unrest
Or lifting lazily on some white crest
His pale foam-feathers for the moon to burn—

Then to my veins I feel new sap return,
Strength tightens up my sinews long grown dull,
And in the old charred crater of the skull
Light strikes the slow somnambulistic mind
And sweeps her forth to ride the rushing wind,
And stamping on the hill-tops high in air,
To shake the golden bonfire of her hair.

This sudden strength that catches up men's souls
And rears them up like giants in the sky,
Giving them fins where the dark ocean rolls,
And wings of eagles when the whirlwinds fly,
Stands visible to me in its true self
(No spiritual essence or wing'd elf
Like Ariel on the empty winds to spin).
I see him as a mighty Terrapin,
Rafting whole islands on his stormy back,
Built of strong metals molten from the black
Roots of the inmost earth: a great machine,
Thoughtless and fearless, governing the clean
System of active things: the winds and currents
Are his primeval thoughts: the raging torrents
Are moods of his, and men who do great deeds
Are but the germs his awful fancy breeds.
For when the winds have ceased their ghostly speech
And the long waves roll moaning from the beach,
The Flaming Terrapin that towed the Ark
Rears up his hump of thunder on the dark,
And like a mountain, seamed with rocky scars,
Tufted with forests, barnacled with stars,
Crinkles white rings, as from its ancient sleep
Into a foam of life he wakes the Deep.
His was the crest that from the angry sky
Tore down the hail: he made the boulders fly
Like balls of paper, splintered icebergs, hurled
Lassoes of dismal smoke around the world,
And like a bunch of crisp and crackling straws,
Coughed the sharp lightning from his craggy jaws.

His was the eye that blinked beyond the hill
After the fury of the flood was done,
And breaching from the bottom, cold and still,
Leviathan reared up to greet the Sun.

Perched on the stars around him in the air,
White angels rinsed the moonlight from their hair,
And the drowned trees into new flowers unfurled
As it sank dreaming down upon the world.
As he rolled by, all evil things grew dim.
The Devil, who had scoffed, now slunk from him
And sat in Hell, dejected and alone,
Rasping starved teeth against an old dry bone.

Before the coral reared its sculptured fern
Or the pale shellfish, swinging in the waves
With pointed steeples, had begun to turn
The rocks to shadowy cities—from dark caves
The deep and drowsy poisons of the sea
Mixed their corrosive strength with horny stones,
And coaxed new substances from them to be
The ponderous material of his bones.
The waves by slow erosion did their part
Shaping his heavy bonework from the mass,
And in that pillared temple grew a heart
That branched with mighty veins, through which to pass
His blood, that, filtering the tangled mesh,
Built walls of gristle, clogged each hollow gap
With concrete vigour, till through bone and flesh
Flowed the great currents of electric sap.
While thunder clanging from the cloudy rack
With elemental hammers fierce and red,
Tempered the heavy target of his back,
And forged the brazen anvil of his head.

Freed from the age-long agonies of birth
This living galleon oars himself along
And roars his triumph over all the earth
Until the sullen hills burst into song.
His beauty makes a summer through the land,
And where he crawls upon the solid ground,
Gigantic flowers, exploding from the sand,
Spread fans of blinding colour all around.
His voice has roused the amorphous mud to life—
Dust thinks: and tired of spinning in the wind,
Stands up to be a man and feel the strife
Of brute-thoughts in the jungle of his mind.
Bellerophon, the primal cowboy, first
Heard that wild summons on the stillness burst,

As, from the dusty mesà leaping free,
He slewed his white-winged bronco out to sea,
And shaking loose his flaming curls of hair,
Shot whistling up the smooth blue roads of air:
As he rose up, the moon with slanted ray
Ruled for those rapid hoofs a shining way,
And streaming from their caves, the sirens came
Riding on seals to follow him: the flame
Of their moon-tinselled limbs had flushed the dim
Green depths, and as when winds in Autumn skim
Gold acres, rustling plume with fiery plume,
Their long hair flickered skyward in the gloom,
Tossed to the savage rhythms of their tune.
Till, far across the world, the rising moon
Heard, ghost-like, in the embered evening sky
Their singing fade into a husky sigh,
And splashed with stars and dashed with stinging spray,
The dandy of the prairies rode away!
That voice on Samson's mighty sinews rang
As on a harp's tense chords: each fibre sang
In all his being: rippling their strings of fire,
His nerves and muscles, like a wondrous lyre,
Vibrated to that sound; and through his brain
Proud thoughts came surging in a gorgeous train.
He rose to action, slew the grumbling bear,
Hauled forth the flustered lion from its lair
And swung him yelping skyward by the tail:
Tigers he mauled, with tooth and ripping nail
Rending their straps of fire, and from his track
Slithering like quicksilver, pouring their black
And liquid coils before his pounding feet,
He drove the livid mambas of deceit.
Oppression, like a starved hyena, sneaked
From his loud steps: Tyranny, vulture-beaked,
Rose clapping iron wings, and in a cloud
Of smoke and terror, wove its own dark shroud,
As he strode by and in his tossing hair,
Rippled with sunshine, sang the morning air.

Like a great bell clanged in the winds of Time,
Linking the names of heroes chime by chime
That voice rolled on, and as it filled the night
Strong men rose up, thrilled with the huge delight

Of their own energy. Upon the snows
Of Ararat gigantic Noah rose,
Stiffened for fierce exertion, like the thong
That strings a bow before its arrow strong
Sings on the wind; and from his great fists hurled
Red thunderbolts to purify the world.

PART TWO

When Noah thundered with his monstrous axe
In the primeval forest, and his boys,
Shaping the timbers, curved their gristled backs,
The ranges rocked and rumbled with the noise.
And as the trees came crashing down lengthwise,
And sprayed their flustered birds into the skies,
That plumed confetti, soaring far and frail,
With such a feathered glory strewed the gale,
That to the firmament they reared a new
But brighter galaxy: and as they flew,
Their rolling pinions, whistlingly aflare,
Kindled in flame and music on the air.
Then, like a comet, the pale Phoenix rose
Blazing above the white star-tusking snows,
And smouldering from her tail, a long white fume
Followed that feathered rocket through the gloom.
To the scared nations, volleying through the calm,
Her phantom was a signal of alarm,
And mustering their herds in frenzied haste,
They rolled in dusty hordes across the waste.
Far in the clouds her fatal meteor shone,
Swelling the turmoil as she hurtled on
Presaging ruin. In his mane of gold
The flaming lion trembled to behold:
And the fierce buffaloes who scorn control
Hushed up the thunder of their hoofs and stole
Like shadows from the plain. Through brakes and thorns
Crashed the wild antelopes with slanted horns:
And tigers, scrawled with fierce electric rays,
Were dimmed to hueless spectres by the blaze.

Skittles to Noah's axe, the great trunks sprawled,
And with the weight of their own bodies hauled

Their screaming roots from earth: their tall green towers
Tilted, and at a sudden crack came down
With roaring cataracts of leaves and flowers
To crush themselves upon the rocks, and drown
The earth for acres in their leafy flood;
Heaped up and gashed and toppled in the mud,
Their coloured fruits poured forth their juicy gore
To make sweet shambles of the grassy floor.
When star by star, above the vaulted hill,
The sky poured out its hoarded bins of gold,
Night stooped upon the mountain-tops, and still
Those low concussions from the forest rolled,
And still more fiercely hounded by their dread
Lost in the wastes the savage tribesmen fled.

Out of its orbit sags the cratered sun
And strews its last red cinders on the land,
The hurricanes of chaos have begun
To buzz like hornets on the shifting sand.
Across the swamp the surly day goes down,
Voracious insects rise on wings that drone,
Stormed in a fog to where the mountains frown,
Locked in their tetanous agonies of stone.
The cold and plaintive jackals of the wind
Whine on the great waste levels of the sea,
And like a leper, faint and tatter-skinned,
The wan moon makes a ghost of every tree.

The Ark is launched; cupped by the streaming breeze,
The stiff sails tug the long reluctant keel,
And Noah, spattered by the rising seas,
Stands with his great fist fastened to the wheel.
Like driven clouds, the waves went rustling by,
Feathered and fanned across their liquid sky,
And, like those waves, the clouds in silver bars
Creamed on the scattered shingle of the stars.
All night he watched black water coil and burn,
And the white wake of phosphorous astern
Lit up the sails and made the lanterns dim,
Until it seemed the whole sea burned for him;
Beside the keel he saw the grey sharks move,
And the long lines of fire their fins would groove,
Seemed each a ghost that followed in its sleep

Those long phantasmal coffins of the deep;
And in that death-light, as the long swell rolled,
The tarpon was a thunderbolt of gold.
Then in the long night-watches he would hear
The whinnying stallions of the wind career.
And to their lost companions, in their flight,
Whine like forlorn cicalas through the night.

By day the sky put on a peacock dress,
And, from its far bewildering recess,
Snowed its white birds about the rolling hull—
The swift sea-swallow and the veering gull
Mixed in a mist of circling wings, whose swoops
Haloed her with a thousand silver hoops;
And from the blue waves, startled in a swarm,
On sunlit wings, butterflies of the storm!
The flying-fishes in their silver mail
Rose up like stars, and pattered down like hail,
While the blunt whale, ponderous in his glee,
Churned his broad flukes and siphoned up the sea,
And through it, as the creamy circles spread,
Heaved the superb Olympus of his head.

Then far away, all in a curve of gold,
Flounced round with spray and frilled with curling foam,
Cleaving the ocean's flatness with its bold
Ridges of glory, rose a towering dome
As the great Terrapin, bulking on high,
Spread forth his huge dimensions on the sky.
Not even Teneriffe, that awful dyke,
When the sun strikes him silver to the spike,
Sends such a glory through his cloudy spray
As did the Flaming Terrapin that day,
Rushing to meet the Ark; with such a sweep
The blue Zambezi rumbles to the deep,
With such a roar white avalanches slide
To strip whole forests from a mountain's side.
But Noah drew his blunt stone anchor in
And heaved it at him; with a thund'rous din
The stony fluke impaled the brazen shell
And set it clanging like a surly bell.
Its impact woke the looped and lazy chain
And rattling swiftly out across the main,

Drawn by the anchor from its dark abode,
Into the light that glittering serpent flowed
Chafing the waves: then as a mustang colt,
Feeling the snaffle, lurches for a bolt—
With such a lurch, with such a frantic rear,
The Ark lunged forward on her mad career,
And the old Captain, with a grip of steel,
Laid his brown hands once more upon the wheel,
Bidding his joyous pilot haul him free
From the dead earth to dare the living sea!
Rowelled by that sharp prow to hissing hate,
The waves washed round her in a dreary spate,
And, as she passed, with slow vindictive swoop
Swerved in to gnash their teeth against the poop:
But like torn Hectors at the chariot wheel,
She dragged their mangled ruins with her keel:
Till puffed by growing rage to greater height,
Their foamy summits towered into the night
So steeply, that it seemed by God's decree
The Alps had all gone marching on the sea,
Or Andes had been liquefied and rolled
Their moonlit ridges in a surf of gold!

O, there were demons in the wind, whose feet,
Striding the foam, were clawed with stinging sleet:
They rolled their eyes and lashed their scorpion tails
And ripped long stripes into the shrieking sails.
High on the poop the dim red lantern glowed,
And soaring in the night, the pale ship rode:
Her shadow smeared the white moon black: her spars
Round wild horizons buffeted the stars,
As through the waves, with icicles for teeth,
She gored huge tunnels, through whose gloom to flee,
And down upon the crackling hull beneath
Toppled the white sierras of the sea!

On fiery Coloradoes she was hurled,
And where gaunt canyons swallowed up the light,
Down from the blazing daylight of the world,
She plunged into the corridors of night
Through gorges vast, between whose giant ribs
Of shadowing rock, the flood so darkly ran
That glimpses of the sky were feeble squibs

And faint blue powders flashing in the pan
Of that grim barrel, through whose craggy bore
The stream compelled her with explosive roar,
Until once more she burst as from a gun
Into the setting splendour of the sun:
Down unimagined Congoes proudly riding,
Buoyed on whose flow through many a grey lagoon,
The husks of sleepy crocodiles went sliding
Like piles of floating lumber in the moon;
Then with the giddiness of her speed elate,
With sails spread like the gold wings of a moth,
Down the black Amazon, cresting the spate,
The smooth keel slithered on the rustling froth:
She moved like moonlight through the awful woods,
And though the thunder hammered on his gong,
Half-dreaming, as beneath their frail white hoods
Sail the swift Nautili, she skimmed along—
Till, raftered by the forest, through whose thatch
The moon had struck its faint and ghostly match,
She saw the monsters that the jungle breeds—
Terrific larvae crawled among the weeds
And from the fetid broth like horrid trees
Wavered their forked antennae on the breeze,
And panthers' eyes, with chill and spectral stare,
Flashed their pale sulphur on the sunless air:
While phosphorescent flowers across the haze,
Like searchlights darted faint unearthly rays:
And gleaming serpents, shot with gold and pearl,
Poured out, as softly as a smoke might curl,
Their stealthy coils into that spectral light
There to lie curved in sleep, or taking flight,
Trundle their burnished hoops across the leaves,
Till the stream, casting wide its forest sleeves,
Heaved out its broad blue chest against the sea,
And from their leafy bondage they were free.
Round the spiked islands, where the wild clouds scale
Flamboyant peaks, and fragrant meadows sweep,
A surf of roses roaring in the gale,
Down to the tufted shingles of the deep,
She passed, and squadrons of huge scarlet crabs
Scampered across the fringes of the land—
Some were as vast as the gnarled baobabs
That hook clawed roots into the desert sand.

There, where the Cyclops herds the mastodon
The sombre crags with lurid splendour shone,
As like a lighthouse towering on the sky,
He rolled the fiery cartwheel of his eye.

On the far headlands, chaired on heaps of bones,
Cannibal kings sat charcoaled on the light,
Till the ship passed, and from their reeking thrones,
They leapt to their canoes in craven flight,
And their slim keels like horses bounded free
To leap the foamy hurdles of the sea;
Like plunging hoofs their paddles spurned the foam,
And, as they rose to crest each frothing comb,
And swung wave-lifted in the whistling air,
The gusty moonlight smouldered on their hair.

Round the stark Horn with buckled masts she clove,
Round the lean fore-arm of the World she drove,
Round the stark Horn, the lupanar of Death,
Where she and that fierce Lesbian, half-aswoon,
Roll smoking in the blizzard's frosty breath,
While, like a skinny cockroach, the faint moon
Crawls on their tattered blanket, whose dark woof
Of knitted cloud shrouds their dread dalliance, proof
To the white archery of the sun, and those
Thin javelins that cold Orion throws.
Round the stark Horn, where bleak and stiffly lined,
Hooked ridges form a cauldron for the wind,
And droning endless tunes, that gloomy sprite
Stoops to his dismal cookery all night,
And with his giant ladle skims the froth,
Boiling up icebergs in the stormy broth,
Brewing the spirits that in sinking ships
Drowned sailors tipple with their clammy lips.

The hurricanes are out!—the whole night long
Humming the cradle-song that lulls the dead,
Where rolling stiffly in a silent throng
Their waif-like corpses on a stormy bed
Toss in their deep deliriums, or sleep,
Lifting pale faces from their restless grave.
Only to sink into a trance more deep
As they loll back upon the pillowing wave.

73

Sailors, so still?—See where the water pales
To milky froth before the whistling gales,
Hear the shrill song, where brawling out of Hell,
Those savage song-birds come to ring your knell,
Hear the low moan, where thunder bursting free,
Mourns for the great tanned nurslings of the sea!
Papooses of the storm! The grey tides lead
Your savage orphaned souls to rest, and thin
Your voices to the rustling of a reed,
Your flesh to vapour, and your horny skin
To spider-threads—and still you lie and dream!
Though the mad hurricanes around you scream,
Twitter and moan, so shrill and piercing-sweet,
That in His stormy turret on the Moon
God even feels His starry rafters beat
Time to the rhythms of the dismal rune
That those ferocious nightingales repeat.

Its four sad candles dripping from their wicks,
The Southern Cross disconsolately swung,
And canted low its splintered crucifix,
While all around the wolfish winds gave tongue,
And, in the silence of the nether shore,
With hateful patience by the hunted ship,
Their slitting fangs and feet that leave no spoor
Raced all night long in drear companionship,
Till, through the shadows of the Southern floe
The awful ghost of Erebus at last
Flowered in the desolation of the snow,
Curling his fiery tresses on the blast:
And the red plumes that rustle in his crest
Tinged the pale icebergs as they loomed abreast
And faintly in the Night's funereal noon
Reared their immense tiaras to the moon:
As they drew near, they hit the dazzled sight
Like ships on fire, and stacked with flaming spears
Old Ocean shone, as swaying through the Night
He rafted up his monstrous chandeliers.
The wild Antarctic lights, ablaze on high,
Rippled their feathered glories up the sky;
As if a phoenix, moulting plume from plume,
Sprinkled his fading splendours on the gloom,
Zigzags of scarlet, combs of silver flame,

Shivering on the darkness, went and came,
And fifty hues, in fierce collision hurled,
Blazed on the hushed amazement of the world!

PART THREE

Now low along the skyline, furred and shagged
As bears, dense clouds in slow contortions dragged
Ponderous bodies, and with clumsy stoop
Came shambling skyward in a sombre troop:
Like quarries shattered out of cliffs, their chaps,
Crammed with resounding cordite, from deep gaps
Exploded thunder, and with jagged spark
Flashed fangs of deathly pallor on the dark.
Drilled by the level sleet, and lashed with spray,
Confounded in the gloom the sailors lay,
Or huddled on the deck their watches kept
Until they whined for sleep: and if they slept,
Sleep was a long dark tunnel demon-scooped
Out of the Night's black rock, in which were grouped
Huge grizzled bats, so aged and so thin
That, as with fruit parched in its wrinkled skin,
About the shrunk pulp of their bodies clung
A loose grey pouch of fur, and as they swung,
Like pennies in a beggar's greasy purse
Their dry bones jingled: and their blood-shot eyes,
The only light, winked redly to disperse
Lank shadows, which the canted stalagmites
Flung forward, dull as falling logs, to fade
Tapering on into the gloom, or rise
Up half-lit walls that lost themselves in shade.

They mourned dead summers: faint remembered flowers
With ghosts of scent and colour filled their hours,
As like poor skeletons, whiskered and lean,
They crouched and prayed for death to intervene:
But life, a scorpion with tenacious hold,
Fastened upon their spirits with the cold
Relentless threat of its infinitude—
And though in that one thought the world seclude
Its fairest hopes, the sense of dying men
Invests it with a nameless horror, when

75

With sight unveiled and sure untingling ear,
Their souls reach out beyond the grave to hear
The whisper of the sea that has no shore.
And all around them as the grim night wore,
The fury of the tempest grew more blind—
Up in the shrouds the whanging of the wind
Wrung from the soulless metal of the wire
A shriek of agony: a sighing fire
Feathered the yards; like devil-rattled dice
Their cold bones shivered, and their fearful wails
Mixed with the hollow grinding of the ice
Above the slatted thunder of the sails.

There in the Night against whose stormy womb
A nameless cape, reared up into the gloom,
With cloudy sperm engendered ghastly forms,
Dread embryos of hurricanes and storms—
Coasting the snows they heard as in a dream
The death-cry and the agony supreme
Of the slow-drowning world. On tongues of flame
Out of the throat of Erebus it came
Drawn through the craggy windpipe of the world:
There where red lava, in Lofodens swirled,
Had funnelled to the sky its stormy flue
The death-gasp of the world came smoking through,
And on the sky's cold glass, frostily strewn,
Lay smeared in phthisic pallor round the moon.
In that great sigh the voices of the world
As in a shroud of ghostly sound were furled.
The souls of Nations, tossed like stormy trees,
With groans and heavy thunder filled the breeze,
And as each race, in travail with its doom,
Sent forth its hollow voice into the gloom,
The flying winds its faint, sad rumour bore
Till all was heard along that dismal shore.
Anarchy, jolted in a rattling car,
Crested the turrets of the storm, and plied
His crackling whip with forked lash to scar
Red weals across the gloom: with frantic stride
His gusty stallions clenched their bits and tore
His whirling spokes along the pitchy rack:
Their gaping nostrils drizzled foam and gore,
And where they passed the gurly sea grew black.

Revolving up in mighty colonnades,
Thick maelstroms propped the dense and sagging shades
With pillared thunder, and with hideous twist,
Corkscrewed by whirlwinds, writhed athwart the mist.

But when their stormy pilot, through the spray,
Like a great ship churning a giant screw,
Rose tilting o'er the waves and thrashed his way
Across the grumbling sea, the weary crew
Forgot their pain and through that night of fear
Sang as they followed in his swift career,
Purged by their agonies of all the dross
Of fear and sloth, their spirits shed their gross
Rags of despair, and as in spangled pride
A python ripples from his shrivelled hide
To ride propelled on wheels of rolling fire,
Their souls emerging from their old attire
Glittered new-sheathed, as if in shining mail,
Steadfast through all the terrors of the gale.
Like moonlight the new splendour of their minds
Flushed their clean limbs: beauty ran all aflare
Through nerve and bone, and whistled in the winds
Threading the burning fibres of their hair.
Fit men they seemed in vigour, brain, and blood,
To mend the swamping havoc of the Flood,
To breed great races and in pride to reign
Throned in the flowering cities of the plain.

But in their absence from the drowning earth,
The sooty Fiend, deep in his mirky firth
Of smoke, upon his throne of roasted bricks,
Bawled his fell triumph far along the Styx,
And Cerberus, his lean three-headed tyke,
Howled his response far down the surly dyke.
Around him then he gathered all his court—
Goblins and apes and elves of every sort.
Huge carrion crows came rasping rusty jaws
Hoarse as the friction of a hundred saws;
Toads pranced about him on their nimble shins
While others sawed their creaking violins:
Gaunt poetesses, shrieking of their sins,
Fresh from the world's asylums, like a rout
Of cackling turkeys, hedged him round about:

While lousy toucans, clanking hollow bills,
Sounded him on, as he bestrode the hills.

Towering like a steeple through the air
He stalks: the cascades of his molten hair
With streams of lava wash his ebon limbs:
His eyes, like wheels of fire with whirling rims,
Revolve in his gaunt skull, from which a tusk
Curves round his ear and glitters in the dusk.
Now he comes prowling on the ravaged earth,
He whores with Nature, and she brings to birth
Monsters perverse, and fosters feeble minds,
Nourishing them on stenches such as winds
Lift up from rotting whales. On earth again
Foul Mediocrity begins his reign:
All day, all night God stares across the curled
Rim of the vast abyss upon the world:
All night, all day the world with eyes as dim
Gazes as fatuously back at him.
He does not hear the forests when they roar
Some second purging deluge to implore,
When cities from his ancient rule revolt,
He grasps, but dares not wield, his thunderbolt.
Sodom, rebuilded, scorns the wilting power
That once played skittles with her tallest tower.
Each Nation's banner, like a stinking clout,
Infecting Earth's four winds, flaunts redly out,
Dyed with the bloody issues of a war,
For hordes of cheering victims to adore.
While old Plutocracy on gouty feet
Limps like a great splay camel down the street;
And Patriotism, Satan's angry son,
Rasps on the trigger of his rusty gun,
While priests and churchmen, heedless of the strife,
Find remedy in thoughts of after-life;
Had they nine lives, O muddled and perplexed,
They'd waste each one in thinking of the next!

Contentment, like an eating slow disease,
Settles upon them, fetters hands and knees;
While pale Corruption, round his ghastly form
Folding the cloudy terrors of the storm,
His shapeless spectre smothered in the blending

78

Of heavy fumes, o'er mirky towns descending,
Swims through the reek, with movements as of one
Who, diving after pearls, down from the sun
Along the shaft of his own shadow slides
With knife in grinning jaws; and as he glides,
Nearing the twilight of the nether sands,
Under him swings his body deft and slow,
Gathers his knees up, reaches down his hands
And settles on his shadow like a crow.
So dread Corruption, over human shoals,
Instead of pearls, comes groping after souls,
And the pure pearl of many a noble life
Falls to the scraping of his rusty knife.
Till glutted with his spoil, like some huge squid,
He reascends, in smeary vapours hid,
And, like those awful nightmares of the deep
When through the gloom propelled with backward sweep
Out of their mirky bowels they discharge
The dark hydraulic jet that moves their large
Unwieldy trunks—back to his secret lair
He welters through the dense miasmal air
In inky vapours cloaking his retreat:
Ever-renewed, his soft and sucking feet
Break from his trunk, and wandering alone,
Grow into forms as ghastly as his own:
Which, in their turn, with equal vigour breed
And through the world disseminate his seed,
Till over every city, grim and vast,
The shadow of a brooding death is cast.

Amphion, whose music planted massive towers
And temples propped on cylinders of stone,
Seems to have risen to this world of ours,
Renounced his lyre, and now to dotage grown,
Across the world in pied pyjamas goes
Fluting a leaky bagpipe with his nose.
A merry piper! Let his flutings rear
New slums and brothels year on dismal year—
Houses where Sickness, wrapped in clogging mist,
Clenches pale children in his bony fist,
And as he sucks his lean and hairy paws,
Slamming the huge portcullis of his jaws,
Enormous lice, like tiger, hog, and bear,

Go crashing in the jungles of his hair.
Let him build ships and muzzle them with dread
To carry death where they might carry bread,
And forge those iron fish, that from their decks,
They launch with thunder bottled in their necks
To strew the waves with limbs of mangled crews.
Let squinting guns command the fairest views,
And giant mills, the temples of despair,
Reared to dull Vulcan and to brutish Mars,
Wolfing huge coals with iron jaws aflare,
Roll their grim smoke to choke the trembling stars!

Youth of the world! pale lichens crawl apace
On Earth's fair limbs and cloud her shining face:
We lie in graves and dungeons and our chains
Are naught but our own sluggard nerves and veins!
See where the Ark, bearded with frost, rolls home,
Her faded ensign trailing in the foam,
Her fiery pilot, with his crest aflare,
Roars out his triumph on the morning air
Rending the gloom: fire-purfled clouds unroll
Their crimson banners round the stormy Pole!

PART FOUR

Thought reared me up to perch upon a crag
That, crooked in heaven like an evil snag,
Shipwrecked the soaring stars, and there I saw,
Clenching his tail within his foamy jaw,
The Kraken, Time, convolved in scaly fold,
Hug the round Earth and girdle her with gold.
Huge throes ran through his equatorial coil,
His spangles, as when water mixed with oil
Whorls rainbows, all disintegrating, swirled
Their violent colours, as whose flames unfurled,
Rippling his scales, all through him seemed to run
A thousand fiery serpents writhed in one,
While future ages rolled into my sight
Spreading prophetic visions on the night.

Far be the bookish Muses! Let them find
Poets more spruce, and with pale fingers wind

80

The bays in garlands for their northern kind.
My task demands a virgin muse to string
A lyre of savage thunder as I sing.
You who sit brooding on the crags alone,
Nourished on sunlight in a world of stone,
Muse of the Berg, muse of the sounding rocks
Where old Zambezi shakes his hoary locks,
And as they tremble to his awful nod,
Thunder proclaims the presence of a god!
You who have heard with me, when daylight drops,
Those gaunt muezzins of the mountain-tops,
The grey baboons, salute the rising moon
And watched with me the long horizons swoon
In twilight, when the lorn hyena's strain
Reared to the clouds its lonely tower of pain.
Now while across the night with dismal hum
The hurricanes, your meistersingers, come,
Choose me some lonely hill-top in the range!
To be my Helicon, and let me change
This too-frequented Hippocrene for one
That thunders flashing to my native sun
Or in the night hushes his waves to hear
How, armed and crested with a sable plume,
Like a dark cloud, clashing a ghostly spear,
The shade of Tchaka strides across the gloom.
Write what I sing in red corroding flame,
Let it be hurled in thunder on the dark,
And as the vast earth trembles through its frame,
Salute with me the advent of the Ark!

Now from their frosty fetters bursting free,
To dare once more the terrors of the sea,
The Ark and her grim pilot churned the foam,
Crested the waves, and hoisted sail for home.
Fierce currents trailed her in their rustling train,
Swishing their silver skirts along the main,
And the grim night, as like proud queens they swayed,
Re-echoed with the great frou-frou they made.
Northward she seethed before the rising gales,
And with the starlight frosted on her sails,
Forth, like a shivering marshfire, flew to skim
With dancing flame the far horizon's rim.
Till in the growing light, tufting the grey

Blank levels with a mead of flowery spray,
The sirens like a sheaf of lilies sprang.
Streaking the depths with faint and snowy limbs,
And in pale constellations, moved and sang
Buoyed on the cadence of their own shrill hymns:
And as the spheres through level ether, bowled
By their own music, chime with tongues of gold—
So to their harmonies the sirens moved
And through the tide their shining orbits grooved.
From their red lips forth rippled on the air
Visible music: shapes with tossing hair
Skipped on the winds, and with a ringing cry,
Rolled in harmonious battle down the sky.

Their tongues like silver hammers beat the air
To crystal armour for those shapes to wear:
Out of each dusty mouthful of the wind
Their throats with vibrant shuttles wove and twined
Glittering robes, by vocal magic wrought
To clothe those airy phantoms of their thought.
And the pale squadrons, clashing through the mists
Tilted by starlight in their windy lists,
Till every one was slain, and the last white
Lingering singer slithered out of sight,
And trailing white foam-roses in her curls,
Sank wavering down to dream among the pearls.

The winds died down: but music filled the sails
With all the speed and beauty of the gales,
And like a nun with twilight-slippered feet,
Sighed on beside the Ark: sounding more sweet
As faintlier it passed, her ghostly tread
Smoothed the untroubled sea, and carpeted
The level mirrors with reflected stars
That floated there like huge white nenuphars,
While dying echoes, leaning to the sail,
Shouldered her onward through the twilight pale.

Cleaving the deep, that miracle of ships,
As smoothly as a psalm divides the lips,
Passed on her way: and still beneath her drawn
Her pale reflection moved, as when the Dawn,

Across the Ocean's polished floors of gloom,
Sweeps her faint shadow with a golden broom.
Smooth as a lover's hand, ere sleep, may slide
O'er the gold sunburn of a woman's side
To drain the moonlight smouldering from her hair—
She stroked the water with her keel, and where
She passed along, it silvered into foam
And burned to take her roving beauty home.
She, whose white form had been the splendid theme
Of chanting hurricanes in their supreme
And wildest inspiration: she, whose white
Virginity appeased the lust of Night,
When in his star-slung hammock, worked with red
Stitches of lightning as with scarlet thread,
She swayed to his embraces as she lay
Dandled in thunder, cosseted in spray!
Now from his couch of terrors borne apart,
She slides alone; the silence on her heart
Weighs down with all the precious weight of gold,
While through the shades, serene and chaste and cold,
She rears aloft her moon-emboldened form,
With child of high endeavour by the Storm.

New signals greeted now the flying ship,
Like lambs the merry waves were seen to skip,
As shepherd winds drove forth their foamy sheep
To rustle through the verdure of the deep:
No more the cruising shark with whispers thin
Through their crisp fleeces sheared his sickle fin
Beside the keel, portending death and woe:
But joyful omens in unceasing flow
Saluted her, as racing with the gales,
She rolled escorted by the rolling whales.

Now far along the skyline, like a white
Signal of triumph through the muffled light,
An Albatross, wheeling in awful rings,
Spanned the serene horizon with his wings,
And towering upward on his scythes of fire,
Smote the thick air, that, strung with beams of light,
Clanged to his harpings like a smitten lyre
Tolling the solemn death-knell of the Night.
Till, rearing higher, he caught the blinding glow

Of sunlight frozen in his plumes of snow,
As his ethereal silver soared to fade
Into the light its own white wings had made,
And, fusing slowly, Albatross and sun
Mingled their two faint radiances in one.

The trancèd crew hailed with a thrilling cry
That snowy sign: but hardly had the sigh
Of the last echo died, when on their sight
Dawned a vast Presence, reddening the Night,
As the old Dragon, from his native slime,
Leviathan, the eldest child of Time,
Projected his gaunt skull upon the gloom,
In tones of thunder prophesying doom.
The blood-red ridges of his drooping gills
Arched the horizon like a range of hills:
In fiery whirlpools, glaring on the skies,
Through blood and foam he churned his rolling eyes
And ruled their long blue rays across the dark
To fix in pallid focus on the Ark.
The sails lit up: the long illumined hull,
Polished with fire, shone like a naked skull,
And the whole ship, in bridal white arrayed,
Stood chiselled out in flame against the shade.

Then the old Serpent, with a voice that fell
Loud as the hammer of a groaning bell
That rocks a steeple—launched his fatal cry
Hounding the laden echoes through the sky:
'Yawn, you great gaps: you starred abysses, yawn
To swill the fiery vintage of the Dawn:
Nature's grim forces heavy with their sleep
Rise up in red rebellion from the deep:
And strong, chained thunders, rifting stone from stone,
Surge underground with subterraneous moan:
Volcanoes, in eruption loud and dire,
Sprawl on the Night with baobabs of fire
And writhe their horrid branches to the Moon
With crackling din. Hark how the shrill Typhoon
Skirls in the towers of Sodom like a cricket
Fiddling her death-dance: splintered like a wicket,
Tall Babel crumples up! The gaunt abyss
Sucks in the darkness with a mournful hiss

84

Gaping for hunger: swirling in its throat
The shadows of a stormy whirlpool float.
Let old Corruption on his spangled throne
Tremble to hear! The jagged rifts of stone
Roar for his mangled carrion: old Earth
Writhes in the anguish of a second birth,
And now casts off her shrivelled hide, to be
The sun's fair bride, as bright and pure as he!
Fleeced like a god in rosy curls of fire
With massive limbs, stiffened by fierce desire,
He leaps, and as she yields her golden thigh,
Gigantic copulations shake the sky!
Old Noah's sons, in pomp and princely pride,
Through all the gardens of the world will ride,
And steepled cities stun the hollow sky
With thunderclaps of bells as they go by,
While at their sides, their stately wives shall pass
Like rays of moonlight on the waving grass,
With flowers twined and scarlet plumes aflare
Like rockets in the midnight of their hair!'

He spoke and sank; and as a cauldron boils
The sea, drawn downward in his horrid coils,
Funnelled a gloomy whirlpit, till the world
Of waters on a single pivot swirled,
And, slowly slackening, once more untwined
Its foamy rings, and rolled before the wind;
But not for long, for the fierce Terrapin,
With one sharp wrench, had snapped the linking cable
And sounded downwards: with a rending din
Half the flat Ocean, tilting like a table,
Rose in a wave, whose long white foamy lip
Slobbered the stars with froth, and sucked the ship
Heavenward on its hoary-whiskered rim.
Dizzy she soared that foaming ridge to skim,
And as a top, whipped into frantic pain,
Scribbles the dust, so on the boiling main
She swirled and eddied: till the snowy crest
Rearing her like the star that gilds the west,
High as the clouds, sank with a strident roar
To strand her on the far, the promised shore!
So a fierce maenad, all her rites performed,
From where among the woods she raved and stormed,

Comes panting, as her frenzy fades away,
To lie sleep-towsled on the moonlit hay.

The dauntless crew, turbulent in their mirth,
Sprang from the decks to stamp the solid earth,
Calling their wives: and as those stately girls
Up from the hatches, wreathed in glimmering curls,
Set foot upon the shore, a sudden surf
Of flowers foamed up to canopy the turf:
They strayed the fields, among the flowers they rolled
Like plundering bees, dabbled with dusty gold,
And watched the light, which trembling as it grew,
Up through the clouds on silver pinions flew.

But the old Terrapin, freed from his load,
On sterner Errands took his lonely road
Over far continents. All through the land
His breath in cyclones pillared up the sand
And drove it on before him. In his ire
He spewed up thunder, and like slots of fire
The loopholed sockets of his eyes betrayed
Their gun-like pupils, as they smeared the shade
With clouds of pitch, and forking through the haze,
Riddled the gloom with fierce electric rays.
Before him floundered havoc, but behind,
Flowers with their scented tassels beat the wind:
After the winter of his wrath he led
A soft atoning Spring and from the red
Cinders he spread before him, as she passed,
Petals and leaves unravelled on the blast,
And tossed their rosy curls like conscious things
Fanned by the glimmering rainbows of her wings.

As a fierce train, maned like a ramping lion
With smoke and fire, thunders on rolling iron
Pounding grim tunes, and grinds with flashing wheel
Rockets of flame from parallels of steel,
And, as the rails curve, shoots from flanks of brass
Tangents of fire to singe the whiskered grass—
So the mad Terrapin, with mighty shoulders
Shunting the hills, moved upon rolling boulders
That, like huge wheels, propelled with savage might,
Revolved their molten globes across the night.

Till far upon a mountain's twinkling spire,
He saw the Devil on his throne of fire
Ruling the world: and launched his fatal shock
Of thunder: as it leapt from rock to rock
Blackening the gulf beneath, and out behind
Its tattered fringes reddened on the wind,
The old Fiend heard it come, and pale with fear
Felt his harsh tresses writhe themselves and rear
Like shocks of wheat. Under his gaudy throne
Avernus yawned with hollow jaws of stone,
As like a skittle to the thunderclap
He sprawled far out into the windy gap,
And, on his baffled pinions loosely flung,
Down through the gloom in huge gyrations swung.
Like a stone toppled from an endless hill,
Compelled as by some fierce insensate will,
Colliding and rebounding from the crags,
Sheer through the deep he tore his whistling rags.
And while through those grim vaults and starless gaps
He rumbled in his hideous collapse,
The damned, each like a grey hook-tailed baboon,
Grown blind with yearning on the fruitless moon,
Hearing his fall, stole forth in rustling troops,
Crammed the cold ledges of the cliff that stoops
Bowed o'er the pit, and there with groping sight
Followed his sinking phantom through the night.
For weary months from cliff to crag he fell,
Until at last the grim recess of Hell,
Stunned by his fall, gave forth a horrid groan
From all its jolted battlements of stone.
And as he dragged his body from the flood,
Pocking deep craters in the sucking mud,
The Dead, like weary snipe, rising on high,
Whined through the gusty pallor of the sky,
And left him there, rending the night with moans,
To nurse the mangled relics of his bones.

After he sank, the clouds from soppy locks
Wrung their last tears the slow descending dew,
The dawn put forth upon the eastern rocks
A milky thigh, and donned a silver shoe,
And through the half-drawn curtains of the mist
Lingered and swayed, a frail somnambulist,

As in fair tresses, on the wind unfurled,
She trawled the rosy morning through the world.

The props of stone that carry the whole night
Upon their shoulders, when her pitchy crows
Perch with faint-spangled wings upon their white
Helmets of frost, and cling with gnarly toes
To their steep Krantzes—in that sudden blaze
Became red beacons, from whose palisade,
Hurled as by some huge fist across the haze,
The Sun burst upward like a red grenade!

PART FIVE

Down on their airy beds,
    As the thin leaves fade on the willows,
The Stars, outwatched, upon cloudy pillows
    Nuzzled their curly heads.
Feathering heaven with ripples of fire,
    The birds stormed up to the sun's dominions,
And the tense air hummed like a silver lyre
    To the stroke of their burning pinions.
Where Behemoth rolled on a river of gold,
    Far down in the valleys below,
The lilies of Africa rustled and beat
Their giddy white flames with the whistle of sleet,
    As they quilted the land with snow.

With the sun on their tansied hair,
    And the wind in their scarlet quills,
White Seraphim rose aflare
    From the tops of the snow-clad hills.
As a song on the strings of a lyre
    Rolls and ripples and dances,
As, surging through forests, a fire
    Shaking its furious lances
Till the bare boughs crackle and twire,
    On wheels of revolving smoke
        In ruin advances—
    So from the eastern skies they broke,
    And with fierce tresses ablaze,
        On billows of fire uprose
To riddle the gloom with the shafted rays
    That they twanged from their golden bows.

88

From the blue vault, with rosy glow,
  In shimmering descent,
Ten thousand angels fell like snow,
Ten thousand tumbling angels went
Careering on the winds, and hurled
Their rainbow-lazos to pursue
  The wild, unbroken world!
Saddled on shooting stars they flew
And rode them down with manes aflare,
Stampeding with a wild halloo,
Gymnastic on the rushing air.
Down on the hills, with a shatter of flame,
The topsy-turvy horsemen came,
The angel cowboys, flaring white,
With lariats twirling, cracking whips,
And long hair foaming in the light,
Vaulting on the saw-backed ridges
Where they tear the sky to strips,
And the rack of thunder bridges
Mountain-tops in dense eclipse:
And the raven cloud, in rout,
Fled like redly smoking ships,
The raven clouds, that with a shout,
Pelting flowers, they beat about
And hounded through the sky.
With ruin sagging from their spars,
Raked by the shrapnel of the stars,
Careering madly by
To roll, torpedoed by a blood-red moon,
Stark crazy on the blast of the typhoon.

And when the champions of the light
Had put their tattered sails to flight,
Star-high they hung above the cliffs suspended,
On scarlet plumes so fierce and splendid
That the sun's beams were turned to running springs
And rippled in the glory of their long spread wings.

Out of the Ark's grim hold
A torrent of splendour rolled—
From the hollow resounding sides,
Flashing and glittering, came
Panthers with sparkled hides,

And tigers scribbled with flame,
And lions in grisly trains
Cascading their golden manes.
They ramped in the morning light,
And over their stripes and stars
The sun-shot lightnings, quivering bright,
Rippled in zigzag bars.
The wildebeest frisked with the gale
On the crags a hunchback mountain,
With his heels in the clouds, he flirted his tail
Like the jet of a silvery fountain.
Frail oribi sailed with their golden-skinned
And feathery limbs laid light on the wind.
And the springbok bounced, and fluttered, and flew.
Hooping their spines on the gaunt karroo.
Gay zebras pranced and snorted aloud—
With the crackle of hail their hard hoofs pelt,
And thunder breaks from the rolling cloud
That they raise on the dusty Veld.
O, hark how the rapids of the Congo
Are chanting their rolling strains,
And the sun-dappled herds a-skipping to the song, go
Kicking up the dust on the great, grey plains—
Tsessebe, Koodoo, Buffalo, Bongo,
With the fierce wind foaming in their manes.

PART SIX

High on the streams of ether, through the void
The angel riders of the air deployed
Their glittering files, as if in one hooped line
Of flame, the far horizons to confine,
And spin a running girdle round the earth—
A belt of fire, in whose expanding girth,
Struck by the sun with one white melting ray,
In all but hue, the ranks dissolved away:
And all their gorgeous dyes, diffusing through
Each other, slowly mingled and withdrew,
Each draining from the glimmering maze its own
Soluble flame, in fluid ease alone
To glide in its own channel: till between
The gold and scarlet ribbons, ran the green,

And in one blaze of watery fire unfurled,
The Rainbow looped the mountains of the world.

Now the Earth meets the Sun: through nerve and limb
Trembling she feels his fiery manhood swim:
Huge spasms rend her, as in red desire
He leaps and fills her gushing womb with fire:
And as he labours, sounding through the skies,
The thunders of their merriment arise!
Now each small seed, thrilled with their mighty lust,
Builds up its leafy palace out of dust
And through its rustling trellises, in springs
Of crystal light, the swift wind flows and sings:
Vibrant with life, each clod of turf, inspired,
Shoots forth a gorgeous flower as if it fired
A rocket at the sky. The steepled trees
Rocked with their great bells clanging in the Breeze
As she passed by with golden locks aswirl,
Of all earth's progeny the fairest girl!
In robes of rustling air she ran to play,
Tripping on trembling lilies all the way,
And the hushed Ocean, puckered into smiles,
Foamed at her feet around its shining isles:
And trees and mountains heard her joyful song
On plumes of towering eagles borne along,
And higher yet, where eagles fear to fly,
Bandied by soaring echoes through the sky.
She slid with white feet planted in a shell
That smoothed the water with its whorlèd prow
Across the deep. Lorn as a midnight bell
Is the remembrance of her beauty now.
The sea's faint marble veined with green and gold
Framed her white image as she glided by:
The clouds, her hoarded fragrances to hold,
Spread seines of tasselled fire across the sky,
And a gay rainbow, curved to catch the pale
Rays of the morning, served her for a sail.

The Flaming Terrapin, his labours done,
Humped like a cloud o'er mountain, crag and field
Rose on the skyline. The far-shooting sun
Splintered its arrows on his armoured shield,
From whose bright dome in sudden ricochets

Recoiling flashed the long reflected rays:
While, rolling his red eyes, a double moon
That lit the hill-sides with a second noon,
He sank to rest. His golden ridges, tiered
Above the foam, now slowly disappeared:
And as clouds roll immense and globed and still
To burst in thunder round a lonely hill,
The slow foam gathered round him: o'er his wild
Mountainous outline, ponderously piled,
It hung one moment, poised in grim suspense,
And then swamped crashing down, and from its dense
Vortex of thunder, with a gradual sweep
Rolled forth in groaning circles on the deep:
Halo on halo, ring on gleaming ring,
Reached out, in long subsiding curves, to fling
The rude waves back and with a foamy crown
Proclaim the Monarch as he sounded down!
Back to the deep he sinks and in a proud
Disintegration, like a raining cloud,
Reversing the grand process of his birth,
Returned his borrowed vigour to the Earth.
That vital fluid, straining through the pores
Of the vast ocean, on the wind upsoars
In rolling clouds that globe around the Sun,
Whence, rinsed as from his fiery curls, they run
In sparkling showers which, teeming in the Earth,
Rouse up the soil to energies of birth,
And shoot new vigour up through giant stems
Wider to spready their leafy diadems,
While from the glad red turf the eager grain
Springs dancing to the silver flutes of rain.
Thence into livelier forms his vigour swims
In fluid grace to beautify the limbs
Of swift wild creatures pasturing in herds,
Through whose lithe bodies, as they graze the plain,
It flows like music—soaping into curds
Of froth along the Koodoo's gusty mane
And slithering in the muscles of the Roan,
And in great Buffaloes, loading with stone
Their horny brows, as with resounding stride
And battering force, in one fierce shock that pulls
The screaming turf up, their huge forms collide
And thunder clothes the battle-angry bulls!

92

Feeding a myriad forms with life and light,
Speed for the race, and courage for the fight,
And Man, triumphant, feels their strength and speed
Thrill through his frame as music through a reed.

Now by each silent pool and fringed lagoon
The faint flamingoes burn among the weeds:
And the green Evening, tended by the Moon,
Sprays her white egrets on the swinging reeds.
Her wings are spangled with the fiery grain
They winnow from the skies, and through the night,
Shoot their soft rays to gild the glistening main:
The swift winds simmer in her ghostly light.
The miser, leaning o'er his greasy hoard,
Cannot her brighter alchemy resist:
The murderer has wiped his grisly sword,
The rusty carbine trembles in his fist;
The trigger turns into a golden pin,
The barrel swings, a lily tall and frail,
And the dark soul, forgetful of his sin,
Walks singing through the terrors of the gale.
Under the feet of pale somnambulists
The thorns are turned to flowers gold and white:
Roses for those sad haunters of the mists
Flame in the secret gardens of the night.
Where each young Hercules, tired of the chase,
Has lain, the earth becomes a mass of flowers:
His pleated muscles and his burning face
Are sweeter to the earth than April showers,
And where he slept the flaming corn aspires
To harp the wind along on golden wires.

High on the top of Ararat alone
Old Noah stood: beneath him faintly blown,
Great aasvogels, like beetles on a pond,
Veered in slow circles o'er the gulf beyond.
The dusk came on: faint shades began to streak
Across the dim cathedral of the peak,
And from his craggy pulpit, the baboon
Rose on the skyline, mitred with the moon.
Over far Edens waved the golden lights
Trailing their gorgeous fringes o'er the heights.
Under the dying splendours of the day,

Rolling around him from his frosty throne,
Ridged with red skies, his mighty kingdom lay
Stretching to heaven. Zone on sweeping zone,
Huge circles outward swirled without a bound,
The world's immense horizons ringed him round,
Receding, merging on until the whole
Creation on the pivot of his soul
Seemed to be wheeling: star on lonely star
Haloed him with its orbit from afar.

He was the axle of the wheel, the pole
Round which the galaxies and systems roll,
And from his being, making months and years
Issued the vast momentum of the spheres.
Those mighty rings seemed but the ripples flung
From his great soul in lofty triumph swung,
An Aphrodite rising from the deep
Of old despairs. Matter's forlorn desire,
Through souls of men, in mighty deeds to leap,
Rose in his soul and crowned itself with fire.
And as the Night, serene and chaste and cold,
Down the faint air on starry pinions rolled,
Loud shouts of triumph through the valleys ran,
And Noah turned to watch, far in the west,
The sun's great phoenix fold her scarlet fan
And sink in ruin from the snowy crest.
There as amid the growing shades he stood
Facing alone the sky's vast solitude,
That space, which gods and demons fear to scan,
Smiled on the proud irreverence of Man.

Night is a Captain hustling up his stars,
Loud is the stumping of their boots of gold
Along the frosty horns and deep-cut scars
Of old bull-mountains sulking in the cold
Vacuums whereto they thrust their snouts to feel
Release from laden pressures or to hear
The humming spokes that twinkle in the wheel
Of many a roving sun. Set in their sheer
Grey brows, the caved unasking eyes with dim
Secrets are slowly filled: wisdom undreamed
Makes heavier their pine-quilled heads where swim
Ponderous fancies: grooved in quartz and seamed

In slate, they pattern their tremendous schemes—
Dead lava scrawled with wrinkled epics: lust
Expressed in stony groins, where distant streams
Dash into puffs of dust
Or trail thin fibres down the slopes to break
And crinkle on the star-bright lake.

Though the dark sky has gathered stormy numbers
Of vultures to be snowed upon my corpse;
Though the weak arc of Heaven warps
Beneath the darkness that encumbers
The night beyond; though we believe the end
Is but the end, and that the torn flesh crumbles
And the fierce soul, rent from its temple, tumbles
Into the gloom where empty winds contend,
In gnat-like vortex droning—what is this
That makes us stamp upon the mountain-tops,
So fearless at the brink of the abyss,
Where into space the sharp rock-rampart drops
And bleak winds hiss?

It is the silent chanting of the soul:
'Though times shall change and stormy ages roll,
I am that ancient hunter of the plains
That raked the shaggy flitches of the Bison:
Pass, world: I am the dreamer that remains,
The Man, clear-cut against the last horizon!'

EPIGRAMS

Holism[1]

The love of Nature burning in his heart,
Our new Saint Francis offers us his book—
The saint who fed the birds at Bondleswaart
And fattened up the vultures at Bull Hoek.[2]

The Land Grabber

*(On a Poet who offered his heart for a handful of
South African Soil)*

The bargain is fair and the bard is no robber,
A handful of dirt for a heartful of slobber.

The Truth about Rhodes

His friends contend that Rhodes is with the saints,
His foes consign him to the Stygian shore;
But all who see him here in Roworth's[3] paints
Will gasp for brandy and dispute no more.

On the Death of a Journalist

Angels received his dying breath,
This last kind act his spirit shrives;
He has done more good by his death
Than could a saint with fifty lives.

[1] From ὅλος = whole; a system of philosophy associated with the name of Jan Christian Smuts.
[2] Where more than a hundred riotous black Africans were killed in 1921 when General Smuts was Prime Minister.
[3] Edward Roworth, a well-known South African painter of portraits and landscapes.

On Professor Drennan's[1] Verse

Who forced the Muse to this alliance?
A man of more degrees than parts—
The jilted Bachelor of Science
And Widower of Arts.

A Temperance Official at the Exhibition of South African Paintings

He stares entranced on sunsets, clouds, and plains,
With rapture eyes the mountains and the rivers—
He's taking tips for diagrams of brains
And charts of swollen livers.

On Some South African Novelists

You praise the firm restraint with which they write—
I'm with you there, of course:
They use the snaffle and the curb all right,
But where's the bloody horse?

On the Same

Far from the vulgar haunts of men
Each sits in her 'successful room',
Housekeeping with her fountain pen
And writing novels with her broom.

[1] Professor of English at the University of Witwatersrand, Johannesburg, at the time of Roy Campbell's association with the magazine *Voorslag*.

Black Magic

('H. Wodson, a name to conjure with in the journalistic
  world.'—*Natal Advertiser*, edited by H. Wodson.)

Sound the dread word. Beelzebub, appear!
For Wodson's name is written on the wall.
The door gapes open, hush, what have we here?
. . . Only a printer's devil after all.

Home Thoughts in Bloomsbury

Of all the clever people round me here
I most delight in Me—
Mine is the only voice I care to hear,
And mine the only face I like to see.

¡Caramba!

Her firm proud flesh admits no queries,
Clear statement which you cannot garble,
Wherein the bust and rump of Ceres
Roll in the rhetoric of marble.

'Poems for Spain' [1]

No sooner had its sales begun
Than all the reds were on the run
And only halted (sink or swim!)
To hack each other limb from limb—
So, once, at least beneath the sun
Poetic Justice has been done!

[1] Edited by Stephen Spender and John Lehmann, London, 1937.

On the Martyrdom of F. García Lorca

Not only did he lose his life
By shots assassinated:
But with a hatchet and a knife
Was after that—translated.

How it Works

Salute the free Utopian State
We fought for. Feed, but do not look.
For each free tuppence-worth of Bait
They charge a dollar on the Hook!

The Beveridge Plan

Through land and sea supreme
Without a rift or schism
Roll on the Wowser's dream—
Fascidemokshevism!

SATIRICAL
AND
POLEMICAL POEMS

The Demos
From *A Song for the People*

I sing the people; shall the Muse deny
The weak, the blind, the humble and the lame
Who have no purpose save to multiply,
Who have no will save all to be the same:
I sing the people as I watch, untamed,
Its aimless pomps and generations roll—
A monster whom the drunken gods have maimed
And set upon a road that has no goal.

*

Funnelled with roaring mouths that gorp like cod
And spit the bitten ends of thick cigars,
This is the beast that dares to praise its god
Under the calm derision of the stars!
When from the lonely beacons that we tend
We gaze far down across the nameless flats,
Where the dark road of progress without end
Is cobbled with a line of bowler hats,

Searching the lampless horror of that fen,
We think of those whose pens or swords have made
Steep ladders of the broken bones of men
To climb above its everlasting shade:
Of men whose scorn has turned them into gods,
Christs, tyrants, martyrs, who in blood or fire
Drove their clean furrows through these broken clods
Yet raised no harvest from such barren mire.

In the cold hour when poets light their tapers
And the tall Muse glides naked to the door,
When by its love, its drinks, its evening papers,
All Babel has been lulled into a snore,
The pious poet in that silence hears
Like some pure hymn uplifting his desires
How Nero's fiddle shrills across the years
And to its music leap the dancing fires.

Overtime

Amongst the ponderous tomes of learning,
Dull texts of medicine and law,
With idle thumb the pages turning
In sudden carnival, I saw,
Revelling forth into the day
In scarlet liveries, nine or ten
Survivors of their own decay—
The flayed anatomies of men:
And marked how well the scalpel's care
Was aided by the painter's tones
To liven with a jaunty air
Their crazy trellises of bones.
In regimental stripes and bands
Each emphasized the cause he serves—
Here was a grenadier of glands
And there a gay hussar of nerves:
And one his skin peeled off, as though
A workman's coat, with surly shrug
The flexion of his thews to show,
Treading a shovel, grimly dug.
Dour sexton, working overtime,
With gristly toes he hooked his spade
To trench the very marl and slime
In which he should have long been laid.
The lucky many of the dead—
Their suit of darkness fits them tight,
Buttoned with stars from foot to head
They wear the uniform of Night;
But some for extra shift are due
Who, slaves for any fool to blame,
With a flayed sole the ages through
Must push the shovel of their fame.

Georgian Spring
From *Adamastor*[1]

Who does not love the spring deserves no lovers—
For peaches bloom in Georgia in the spring,
New quarterlies resume their yellow covers,
Anthologies on every bookshelf sing.
The publishers put on their best apparel
To sell the public everything it wants—
A thousand meek soprano voices carol
The loves of homosexuals or plants.
Now let the Old Cow perish, for the tune
Would turn the fatted calf to bully beef:
We know, we know, that 'silver is the Moon',
That 'skies are blue' was always our belief:
That 'grass is green' there can be no denying,
That titled whores in love can be forgot—
All who have heard poor Georgiana sighing
Would think it more surprising were they not:
As for the streams, why, any carp or tench
Could tell you that they 'sparkle on their way'.
Now for the millionth time the 'country wench'
Has lost her reputation 'in the hay'.
But still the air is full of happy voices,
All bloody: but no matter, let them sing!
For who would frown when all the world rejoices,
And who would contradict when, in the spring,
The English Muse her annual theme rehearses
To tell us birds are singing in the sky?
Only the poet slams the door and curses,
And all the little sparrows wonder why!

[1] 'Adamastor' was the name given by the sailors of Vasco de Gama to the fierce, storm-wreaking demon supposed to haunt the Cape of Good Hope. It is described in the fifth *Lusiad* of Luiz de Camões. Campbell chose the name as the title of a collection of poems published in 1930.

Junction of Rails: Voice of the Steel

Cities of cinemas and lighted bars,
Smokers of tall bituminous cigars,
Whose evenings are a smile of golden teeth—
Upon your cenotaphs I lay this wreath
And so commend you to the moon and stars.

For I attain your presence in the dark
Deriding gossip Reuter's twittered spark
And reach you rails that, swifter in career,
Arrive as due as they depart from here—
I am a tour on which the hours embark.

Through me the moon, in ruled meridian steel,
Unwinding journeys from a burnished reel,
Stitches the world with threads of fire: each clue,
Pulleyed with rolling-stock as webs with dew,
A nerve for sleeping capitals to feel.

Their life-blood circulating in my veins,
With runnelled iron I irrigate the plains
And spider touring metal through the rock,
While to the same tentacular tick-tock
My scarecrow signals semaphore their trains.

Under this bleak mechanical display
I screen an inward knowledge, when the day
X-rays the fingers of my open hand
Over the chess-board acres of the land
Whose towns are shifted peons in the play.

Progress, the blue macadam of their dream,
Its railed and shining hippodrome of steam,
Glazed by cool horsepower, varnished clean with wheels,
Filming their destiny in endless reels,
Defers the formal ending that they scheme.

They greet each other in these gliding cars,
Read the same nightly journal of the stars,
And when the rail rings I can hear the bells

Ringing for dinner in the world's hotels
And after that that the closing of the bars.

Though they have taught the lightning how to lie
And made their wisdom to misread the sky
I told their pulses: through my ringing loom
Their trains with flying shuttles weave a doom
I am too sure a prophet to defy.

And when they jargon through the wind and rain
Breathing false hopes upon a frosty pane,
I hear the sad electrocuted words
Thud from the wires like stiffly-frozen birds
That warming hands resuscitate in vain.

The De Profundis of each canine hell
Voices their needs in its voluptuous swell:
While from the slums the radio's hollow strain
From hungry guts ventriloquizing pain
Belies them, as it sobs that all is well.

Then like a flawless magnet to the fact
Into my secret knowledge I attract
Their needles of dissimulated fear
Whose trembling fingers indicate me here
The focus of their every mood and act.

What hopes are theirs, what knowledge they forgo
From day to day procrastinating woe—
I, balancing each project and desire,
Funambulize upon my strands of fire
Too many aspirations not to know.

I am the plexus of their myriad schemes,
And were I flesh the ruin would undo me
Of all the purposes they sinew through me,
Of thwarted embassies, and beaten teams,
And home-returning honeymoons as gloomy.

How shrill the long hosannas of despair
With which those to-fro scolopendras bear,
Statesmen to conferences, troops to war—
All that concerted effort can restore
Like rattled cans to porters of despair!

But in the waiting-room where Time has beckoned
His vanguard, every moment must be reckoned
And fierce anticipation push the clock
Though for each same reiterated second
The whole world swing its pendulum of rock.

Far on the plain my waving pennons stream,
In the blue light the white horsetailing steam:
Or where they storm the night with rosy cirrus—
Armoured incendiary, plumy Pyrrhus!
Through palaces of ice where eagles scream.

From fog-red docks, the sink of rotting drains,
Where, tipsy giants, reel the workless cranes:
Where in dead liners, that the rust attacks,
Sprung decks think back beyond the saw and axe,
And masts put on the green of country lanes—

I tentacle the news: relay the mails:
And sense the restive anger that prevails
Wherever shafts descend or girders rise:
And day and night their steel-to-steel replies
Hum in my bolts and tingle in my rails.

These tons of metal rusting in the rain
(Iron on strike) are singing one refrain:
Let steel hang idle, burning rust devour,
Till Beauty smile upon the face of Power
And Love unsheathe me from the rust again ...

My rails that rove me through the whispered corn
Bring me the tidings of a world unborn:
My sleepers escalading to the skies
Beyond the far horizons seem to rise
And form a Jacob's ladder to the morn.

And I have often thought by lonely sidings—
What shepherd or what cowboy in his ridings
Forges the Sword so terrible and bright
That brings not peace, but fury of delight,
And of whose coming I have had the tidings.

They are the tidings of a world's relief:
My aching rails run out for their belief
To where a halted Star or rising Crescent
Above a byre or sheepfold hangs quiescent,
And meditation reaps the golden sheaf—

The joy that veld and kopje thrice restored
To that bleak wilderness the city horde—
When once the living radios of God,
By ravens fed, the lonely places trod,
And talked with foxes, and with lions roared.

A sword is singing and a scythe is reaping
In those great pylons prostrate in the dust,
Death has a sword of valour in his keeping
To arm our souls towards the future leaping:
And holy holy holy is the rust
Wherein the blue Excaliburs are sleeping!

Warrior's Reward

From *The Soldier's Reply to the Left-Wing Poet*

O well may he weep for the soldier,
Who weeps at a guinea a tear,
For although his invention gets mouldier,
It keeps him his job in the rear.
When my Mrs the organ is wheeling
And my adenoids wheeze to the sky,
He will publish the hunger I'm feeling
And rake in his cheque with a sigh:
And when with a trayful of matches
And laces, you hawk in the street,
O comrades, in tatters and patches,
Rejoice! since we're in for a treat:
For when we have died in the gutter
To safeguard his income and state,
Be sure that the Poet will utter
Some beautiful thoughts on our Fate!

From *The Wayzgoose*

In 1926 Roy Campbell, now a celebrity, owing to the success of *The Flaming Terrapin*, returned to South Africa, where in association with the novelist William Plomer he launched a monthly literary magazine called *Voorslag* ('Whiplash'). Its purpose, as he explained in a prospectus, was 'not to interest amateurs of *le vice Anglais*, but to sting with satire the mental hindquarters of the bovine citizenry of the [South African] Union.' It was also intended to provide a much-needed outlet and medium of communication for promising South African writers.

The first issue of *Voorslag* appears to have been a literary success. It contained among other things Campbell's poem *The Albatross* (see page 174), an essay *On Beauty and Nature* by the philosopher-politician, Jan Christian Smuts, and a dissertation on the work of Cézanne by the well-known painter, Edward Roworth. The second issue, however, included an article by Plomer on the explosive race question, which provoked an uproar large enough to frighten those who had been backing the magazine financially. In the third issue Campbell announced his resignation as editor, and soon afterwards returned to Europe.

The Wayzgoose, published in 1928, is his first long satirical poem, written in the heat of his fury, frustration and disgust over the *Voorslag* episode. The following excerpts from it will illustrate the savage quality of his wit.

A wayzgoose in former times was a feast given by a master printer to apprentices who had served out their indentures and were about to assume the status of journeymen. The name seems to have derived from the fact that it was traditional to serve as the main dish a goose specially fattened for the occasion. Later the word was applied to the annual outings or celebrations of members of the printing trade. In South Africa it seems to have been adopted to designate a convocation of journalists. In his imaginary wayzgoose, however, Campbell pretended to assemble for purposes of satirical slaughter professors and other intellectuals as well as writers, artists and editors.

Botanocracy

South Africa, renowned both far and wide
For politics and little else beside:
Where, having torn the land with shot and shell,
Our sturdy pioneers as farmers dwell,
And, 'twixt the hours of strenuous sleep, relax
To shear the fleeces or to fleece the blacks:
Where every year a fruitful increase bears
Of pumpkins, cattle, sheep, and millionaires—
A clime so prosperous both to men and kine
That which were which a sage could scarce define;
Where fat white sheep upon the mountains bleat
And fatter politicians in the street;
Where lemons hang like yellow moons ashine
And grapes the size of apples load the vine;
Where apples to the weight of pumpkins go
And donkeys to the height of statesmen grow,
Where trouts the size of salmon throng the creeks
And worms the size of magistrates—the beaks;
Where the precocious tadpole, from his bog,
Becomes a journalist ere half a frog;
Where every shrimp his proud career may carve
And only brain and muscle have to starve.
The 'garden colony' they call our land,
And surely for a garden it was planned:
What apter phrase with such a place could cope
Where vegetation has so fine a scope,
Where *weeds* in such variety are found
And all the rarest *parasites* abound,
Where pumpkins to professors are promoted
And turnips into Parliament are voted?
Where else do men by vegetating vie
And run to seed so long before they die?

What wonder if, assuming portly airs,
Beetroots should sit in editorial chairs,
Or any cabbage win the critics' praise
Who wears his own green leaves instead of bays!
What wonder then if, as the ages pass,
Our universities, with domes of glass,

Should to a higher charter prove their claims
And be exalted to tomato-frames,
Whose crystal roofs should hatch with genial ray
A hundred mushroom poets every day;
Where Brussels scientists should hourly sprout
And little shrubs as sages burgeon out;
Where odes from beds of guano should be sprung
And new philosophies from horses' dung?
Wisdom in stones some reverend poet found,
But here it is as common as the ground—
Behold our Vegetable Athens rise
Where all the *acres* in the Land are *wise*!

Statesmen-philosophers with earnest souls,
Whose lofty theories embrace the Poles,
Yet only prove their minds are full of Holes,[1]
And public orators, each one of whom
Had talked both Boer and Briton to their doom,
And slain, the feat of Samson to surpass,
Whole thousands with the jawbone of an ass—
The pale blue Naiads from their streams of ink
With pale blue stockings, such as never shrink,
With pale blue spectacles and pale blue stays,
And pale blue insight into human ways—
Nymphs of the novel, pert and picturesque,
And wooden hamadryads of the desk.

South African Journalism

Over the trades the journalists exult
And unemployment is the sad result.
You hoary sires, who send your sons to schools,
To learn good English and to keep its rules,
While deep into their wooden skulls, like tintacks,
The masters hammer in the rules of syntax—
What boots this weary labour and expense
Save to pervert them into common sense?
Save time and labour! teach them but to bore,
Cradle their youth in journalistic lore,

[1] See note, page 99.

114

Teach them to walk in Dullness' narrow way,
And never from Tautology to stray,
Feed them on Kipling, nourish them on *Punch*—
And in their works the World will wrap its lunch!

Alas, good souls, with what dyspeptic ire
You boast your race and patriotic fire!
Show first that English blood you love to brag
And prove the spirit—if you claim the Flag.
Is yours the giant race in times of yore
That bred a Dryden, or a Marvell bore?
Are you the English, you, that groaning sit
Shot through and riddled by a Dutchman's wit?
Is it so English under Tielman's[1] blows
To whine your impotence in feeble prose,
Your Pegasus a mule, your Muse a trull,
And is it to be English—to be dull?
What are your threats of battles that impend
And what would these avail you in the end?
Rush headlong forth for politics to die,
Go, sacrifice tame mutton for a lie,
Choose bricks and bats, choose anything but Wit,
The only thing that helps your cause a whit!
Rather with Tielman would I stand in yoke
Than rank with you in impotence and smoke,
For to his ignorance is wit suspended
Like an old Tomcat with its tail appended,
But your own ignorance is purely Manx
And has no stump to tally with its shanks.
You journalists with righteous wrath who swell
To see a brother turned into a smell—
Be warned by me and his own dreadful fate
Who dies your many sins to expiate—
Sooner with your own pens a lion assail
Or pick a sleeping mamba in the tail,
Than dare the great Apollo to abuse
Or squirt one drop of ink upon the Muse.
Sooner your own vile ink in buckets swill
And swallow both the paper and the quill—
Than dare, though journalists you be, our curse,
Which still can turn you into something *worse*.
We poets will forgive you all we can

[1] Tielman Roos, an Afrikaans Appeals Judge and Nationalist politician.

With you the dog 'is father to the man';
'Tis Nature's whim that dogs, when taken short,
Still to the loftiest monument resort,
And oft we shrug and often we are mute
When you our sacred monuments pollute:
Dogs and colonials are in this alike—
One law suffices both for man and tyke—
But dogs are pleased with humble walls at times
And lift their legs unconscious of their crimes,
Yet what colonial would not run a mile
Might he some shining edifice defile?

And one was there whom I had seen before,
Full high in anticlimax he could soar
And probe 'behind the button'[1] Nature's lore!
Forgive me, Statesman, that I have purloined
This deathless phrase by thine own genius coined,
Seek on, 'Behind the BUTTON', in the Void—
Until you come upon the works of Freud!
Statesman-philosopher! I shake thy hand—
All tailors envy thee throughout the land
Whose BUTTON-HOLISM, without reverse,
Undoes the Trousers of the Universe!
Long be thy wisdom honoured, and thy race
Renowned for flinging smuts in 'Beauty's' face!
Long may thy race perform its glorious part
And scatter smuts on every work of art:
Let Plomer's art as mutty filth be banned—
And own us prophets in our native land!

The South African Muse

'Twas She who first the flames of Genius lit
In Herman's[2] 'Guide Book to the Infinite',
Wherein the sage records and much admires
How his great-grandmother detected fires,
And of her telepathic powers doth tell,
Which he confuses with her sense of smell.

[1] The phrase is from an essay by General Smuts. See note, page 99.
[2] Louis Herman, a Cape Town schoolmaster, author of *A History of the Jews in South Africa*. Apparently the 'Guidebook to the Infinite' existed only in Campbell's imagination.

For when in suffocating fumes she woke
And found her room half-hidden in the smoke,
Some 'supernormal power', he says, was nigh her
And warned her that the building was on fire!
'Tis She who when our Scots professors woo
Sadly reminds them of their 'mither's broo',
'Tis She who makes our nature poets melt
With yearning for the bleak and barren veld,
Whither, though trains from every junction puff,
They never venture—sensibly enough!
Inspired by Her the lofty Drennan sprung
To write his poems—yet remain unhung:
'Twas due to Her—a couple rather odd,
That Drennan in the garden walked with God.
'Twas She who breathed the Theory Holistic,
And turned a general into a mystic.

In ink invisible She dyed her charms
And dimmed the yellow freckles on her arms:
Colonial grace on all her motions hung
And wit colonial tittered on her tongue—
She seemed, as there She tossed her wanton curls,
The prototype of all colonial girls,
For like a V upturned, stork-like and thin,
Her long straight legs forked downward from her chin;
Had there been room for one to intervene,
Her body like a goitre would have been—
But what of that? Colonial poets tell
That beauty only in the Soul can dwell
(Poor devils! they are right—at least as far
As goes their knowledge of what 'women' are):
A head, two shins, a knot of withered hair,
Suffice to make colonial 'women' fair.
The body is indecent: She had none
Nor would have deigned to own it had she one.
But ah! her Soul's dimensions to report—
Elephantiasis comes far too short!
Like some huge Zeppelin, its inflated cyst
Flew far above and hovered in the mist.
Her two long teeth protruded like a vole's—
In women still the sign of ardent souls,
And at her shoulders played, like eagle's wings,
Two wild banana leaves attached by strings.

What's that within your hands—is that the Pen,
Once sharp, and once the implement of Men—
Was this, ye gods, the dainty Whistler's foil
When he from Ruskin let a tun of oil,
And, like a swordfish round a whale astreak,
Deep through the yielding blubber shot his beak?
Was this the huge harpoon that Marvell bore
To fish the corps of Holland to the shore?
Was this the boomerang that Dryden threw
To crumple Flecknoe as I crumple you?
Alas, and has it come to this strange use?
Its stem all rusty and its point obtuse.
In Wodson's[1] hand it scratches like a pin—
So rasps the cricket with his horny shin,
And, wrapped around it like a woollen bib,
Lo! Jubb's[2] soft hand, perspiring, plies the nib.

White and Black

Alas, poor Tielman, what is he to blame?—
A Locust at the word of God he came,
With huge moustaches, like antennae curled,
And paper wings to swoop across the world.
He spares your gum-trees and he spares your crops,
But on your testimonials he drops,
He chews certificates, your chits he gnaws,
And plays the devil with your paper laws:
Your flagstaffs like banana-leaves are ripped,
Your notice-boards like mealie-stems are stripped,
Acres of paper desolated lie,

[1] Editor of the Natal *Advertiser*.
[2] 'Polybius Jubb': Campbell's name for Maurice Webb, an English Fabian socialist and vegetarian who migrated to Durban and was subsequently named business manager of *Voorslag*. The poet disliked him intensely and ridiculed him often in verse. A limerick, entitled 'The Death of Polybius Jubb', goes

> He died in attempting to swallow—
> Which proves that, though fat, he was hollow
> For in gasping for space
> He swallowed his face,
> And hadn't the courage to follow.

And groans of angered citizens reply.
Alas, poor Durbanites, which will you choose,
Which of the dread alternatives refuse,
This is the ultimatum that you shirk,
The awful question—Poverty or Work?
Work, that can turn a draper to a Man
And give a human accident a plan.
Work, that could make the sugar-planting race
Stand up and look a black man in the face!
Is it the sign of a 'superior race'
To whine to have 'the nigger kept in place'?
Where is his place save in his strength and sense,
And will he stand aside for impotence,
Does Evolution wait for those who lag
Or curtsy to a cheap colonial Flag?
Is this 'White Labour'—lolling on this stool,
Fed by a black with every needful tool,
The white man sits and uses but his hands,
The black man does the thinking while he stands:
Five years in long apprenticeship were passed
Ere, fit to loaf, the white emerged at last,
And yet in kicks and blows the black must pay
Unless he learns the business in a day.

The Poet's Triumph

True poesy admits no curb at all
Though judges bellow, and though lawyers bawl;
Down on the gravest judge, as on a child,
My muse has looked, and as a parent, smiled:
For rhyme above the heads of monarchs sails
And wit outlasts the concrete of the gaols.
Then hear the damned sedition that I sing,
A poet, though in rags, is thrice a king,
Who dares the world, without an army, face
And kick a mongrel town into its place!
Jostling with emperors, an outlaw gay,
Shouldering paunchy statesmen from his way,
Along the sounding thoroughfares of time
He swaggers in the clashing spurs of rhyme,

And all around him throng, with forms divine,
His gay seraglio of Muses Nine,
Those strapping girls whose love, to say the least,
Would make a rabid Mormon of a priest.

Apparition

A *poet*, on his way to bathe, had stumbled
Nude, on the gathering: the heavens rumbled:
Chaste ladies screamed as at a hippogriff
And even on roast fowls, though cold and stiff,
The parsons' noses gave a little sniff:
Forth from the bush that awful vision peered
And like a flambeau flared his ginger beard.
A Tarzan on the fringes of the wood,
Hairy and huge, gorilla-like he stood:
He showed his shaggy face and hairy chest
But wild banana-leaves concealed the rest.
Some gasped, some stared, but it is fair to say
The lady-writers turned the other way.[1]
He gave a growl, the journalists—a start,
Then wistfully they turned them to depart.
Whatever type of bores they may have been,
At least they proved they were not Gadarene,
Those had the sense to drown themselves: but these
Stole meekly off between the darkening trees.

From *The Georgiad*

Campbell, who preferred the society of sailors, fishermen, cattle-
herders and even prize-fighters to that of other writers—though he
excepted a few firm friends like Wyndham Lewis and the Sitwells—

[1] The allusion here is to 'Portraits in the Nude', a short story by Plomer, included
in the collection called *I Speak of Africa*. According to Campbell, some puritanic
South Africans were scandalized by the title, but he was doubtless exaggerating.
He also alleged that the story was bowdlerized by the editors of a Natal magazine
in which it was first published.

came to despise the London literary world and what he considered its artificialities, commercialization and pretentious posturings. He believed, or affected to believe, that it was riddled with effeminacy. A romantic individualist, a hater of industrialism and the egalitarian tendencies of times, he particularly detested the Fabian intellectuals and other social reformers. A fancier of horseflesh and bullflesh and of large animals generally, the middle-class Englishmen's worship of small pets, especially dogs—or tykes, as he liked to call them—excited his derision. He poured out his scorn in another long and libellous satire modelled on the *Dunciad* of Pope, as *The Wayzgoose* seems to have been modelled on Dryden's *MacFlecknoe*.

The Georgiad, written during Campbell's years among the fisher-folk and cattle traders of Mediterranean France and published in 1931, was widely read in England, in many cases perhaps with almost as much malicious delight as the poet found in writing it, and it received some notice, favourable and otherwise, in the United States; but the excerpts given here will show why it cost him whatever favour his work may previously have found among the Bloomsbury set. Later Campbell was to boast that the poem, which covers more than forty pages of ten-point type, had already become a classic. In a sense he was right; but now that many of his victims are dead and largely forgotten, the whole of *The Georgiad*, like that of *The Dunciad*, is of interest mainly to students of the period concerned. (Those who may wish to read it in full, however, will find it in the first volume of *Collected Poems* published by The Bodley Head in 1949 and in the volume of *Selected Poems*, published in 1955 by Henry Regnery Company, Chicago.)

Invocation

Since Georgians are my theme why should I choose
Any but the most broadly smiling muse?
Inspire me, Fun, and set my fancy gliding,
I'll be your Graves and you my Laura Riding,[1]
Or since the metaphor has set you frowning,
That other Robert and his Mrs, Browning.
Let us commune together, soul with soul,
And of our two half-wits compound a whole:

[1] Evidently an allusion to the collaboration of Mr Graves and Miss Riding in several books of criticism and in a publishing venture on the island of Majorca.

Swap brains with me 'for better or for worse'
Till neither knows which writes the other's verse:
Think all my thoughts, though they be stale and few,
And when you think I'll think the same as you.
For when 'two minds without a single thought,
Two hearts that beat as one', in touch are brought,
There's nothing for it but to burst all fetters
And form a joint Hermaphrodite-of-letters.

'Androgyno'

So spoke a Poet to his willing Muse,
And soon as told the blissful change ensues;
Now fully armed the direst foe to meet,
This new 'Orlando' flounces to his feet,
And with a virginally vulpine air,
The hair-pins falling from his frowsy hair,
First meets his own approval in the glass,
Then tries his voice, to see if it will pass,
And finds the organ, beat it if you can,
Able to lisp as sweetly as a man,
Or roll far down into as deep a bass
As any lady-writer in the place.
It was a voice of 1930 model
And in a Bloomsbury accent it could yodel
Between its tonsils drawling out long O's
Along its draughty, supercilious nose:
Or coo in satire gentle and polite
To fill the soul of Humbert[1] with delight:
But then alas, changing its tone and mood,
It could at times be quite unkind and rude,
And give a growl the stoutest heart to scare,
Or startle Humbert from his dreamy stare
Among the weeping willows of his hair,
Whereon, I only wish it for the best,
He'd sometimes hang his harp up for a rest.
His voice thus tried, our hero turns about

[1] Humbert Wolfe (1885–1940), author of *The Uncelestial City*, *The Upward Anguish* and other books of verse. Also known for his encouragement of younger poets.

And in the mirror, with a joyful shout,
Seeing his new physique, decides to patent
The whole machine, in which, so far from latent,
Both sexes rampantly dispute the field
And at alternate moments gain or yield.

*

A child could see he was no tame result
Of boarding-school, or 'varsity, or cult,
No mass-reaction from a moral reign,
But the live product of a poet's brain
Pumped full to bursting of divine afflatus,
And with a fifty-horsepower apparatus.
No cruel War was midwife to his state,
No youthful accident had warped his fate,
His feelings worked upon no Freudian plan
In which the child is father to the 'Nan',
Nor would he dogmatize his pet perversions
With psycho-analytical assertions.
His sexual foundations were not laid
In the Scout Movement or the Church Brigade,
He had no high ideals or moral saws
With which to break the old Hebraic laws,
With Edward Carpenter[1] he had no patience
Nor from the 'Sonnets' would he make quotations,
No Lesbian governess had got the start of him
Or tampered early with the female part of him:
Even his misdemeanours, the most sooty,
Were more of a diversion than a duty:
He was not even member of some Church-
Society for sexual research,
Like Bertrand Russell or the wise MacCarthy[2]—
For frowsiness his disrespect was hearty:
He read no text-books: took himself for granted
And often did precisely what he wanted:
Taking his pleasures in and out of season,
He gave for his perversity no reason,
But leaped alive (as you have seen) in rhyme
And forged ahead to have a happy time.

[1] Poet and essayist; social and sexual reformer; author of *Love's Coming of Age* (1844–1929).

[2] Desmond MacCarthy, eminent critic and literary editor of *The New Statesman*; a strong champion of Campbell's poetry.

The Literary Springtide

Now hawthorn blooms above the daisied slope
Where lovelorn poets after milkmaids grope,
Or troop whore-hunting down the country lanes
With flashing spectacles and empty brains,
To hang their trousers on the flowering spray
And sport with lousy gypsies in the hay.
Here Bulbo comes his amorous hours to pass
Tickled by spiders on a tump of grass:
And sure, what blushing milkmaid would despise
Humpty's great belly and protruding eyes,
Who in his verses plainly has revealed
That when he ogles every maid must yield!
If they should fail to win the joys they sing
Or get a cuff to make their ear-drums ring,
It makes no difference, they forgive the crime
And finish off the merry feat in rhyme—
Editors are the safest go-betweens—
All maids are willing in the magazines:
More lonely hearts are linked by the Reviews
Than by the 'Link' of 'Matrimonial News',
And any one who feels a trifle flighty
Can get off in 'The London Aphrodite',
Where upon every page, always in 'hay'
These donkeys jack their mares the livelong day.

*

Others in London sigh with equal force
For Sussex downs and whiffs of Kentish gorse,
And though the trains puff out from morn till eve,
Vastly prefer to stay at home and grieve.
Some to the pubs, muffled like bolshies, go
To sink themselves into a fit of woe:
These are the guys that find the world forlorn
And wish (correctly) they had not been born:
Blaspheming all the universal plan
Because their tart prefers some better man,
Each loves to sit there and astronomize
The floating specks that swim before his eyes,

His world a dream, his life a trickle of stout,
With sleeps between, and death for chucker-out.

The Cynophiles

Here, too, the spirit of the spring exults
In wilder fêtes and more outlandish cults:
For as all nations have their sacred anibal
(Excuse my cold)—Christian as well as cannibal:
The wild Australians, their Kangaroo,
And Hottentots, their mantis—both 'taboo':
The valiant Spaniards (Mithras' fiery breed)
Their angry Bull: the Bedouin their steed:
Their feathered snake—the Zulus and the Aztecs,
And the bad Afghans their connubial 'pasteques';
So the meek Georgians have their tribal god
And in their language, which is far from odd,
Spell it with the same letters (D, O, G,)
As, backwards, spell the true Divinity . . .
So hither flock (amongst the other Boobies)
The priests and high-priestesses of Anubis,[1]
And hither all their shaggy minions bring
Till with their howls the woods and valleys ring.
Here grim 'Canute' whose one besetting vice
Is biting polar-bears on bergs of ice
(So says the Georgian poetess in song)
Chief of the canine army, trots along:
Behind him spreads the never ending throng
Of all the bow-wows, poodles, tykes, and curs
That Georgian poets ever hymned in verse,
And from their throats as weird a music flows
As ever from their masters' lips arose.
Now, while their owners do the same indoors,
Across the lawn they shank it on all fours,
To argue, fight, and copulate, and piddle
Around the sacred lamp-post in the middle
Which was erected by the joint subscription
Of Georgian writers, with the just inscription,
'Let no hard heart a passing tear refuse
To the dumb martyrs of the Georgian Muse'.

[1] The dog-headed god of the Egyptians.

Why should I name the whole illustrious throng
Each Argus and Cuchulainn,[1] who have long
Been famous in the annals of our song?
But of the chief cynolaters who there
Foregathered for devotion, psalm, and prayer,
First Bottomley[2] (Horatio) was seen,
With pet on leash, to pace the shaven green,
And oft in verse addressed the faithful 'Toby'
That bit his poor old Muse with hydrophobie.
Next him Jack Squire[3] through his own tear-drops sploshes
In his great, flat, trochaical goloshes,
And far behind him leaves a spoor of mud
To sprout a thousand lilies of Malud—
Now as he would exalt to deathless Fame
His vanished Lycidas, 'Willie' by name,
And to the dead man's pet his grief expresses,
Outslobbering the bulldog he caresses,
Like some strange Orpheus for Eurydice
Inciting Cerberus to sympathy.
The patient monster as he listens drops
A sympathetic trickle from his chops,
And both together mix the mutual moan,
Squire for the dead, and Fido for a bone.
Partners in grief, in watery tourney vie
The rheumy jowl and the poetic eye,
While with its tail for baton, keeping time,
The poet wags his mangy stump of rhyme.

*

Ah Willie, Willie, better have been hung
Than exorcized thus in the canine tongue,
What had you done to Squire save live and die
The apple, nay, the onion, of his eye?
May some kind god my funeral defend
From such a poet and from such a friend,

[1] Hero of the Red Branch, or Ulster, cycle of Irish mythology. The name means 'Culann's Hound', bestowed on him at the age of six, when having slain with his bare hands a ferocious watch dog belonging to the armourer Culann, he offered himself as a substitute.

[2] Editor during First World War of the ultra-jingoistic newspaper *John Bull*. In 1922 he was convicted of grave frauds and sentenced to prison where he wrote the sentimental poems to which Campbell alludes.

[3] Sir John Squire, editor of the *London Mercury*; minor poet best remembered for his ingenious parodies.

Who by his comrade's death is less put out
Than by his pity for a 'waggling' trout,
And should one near my coffin show his face
May some wing'd Bulldog of Cerberean race,
With rabid fangs and fiercely wagging stump,
Be there to tear the trousers off his rump!

The Lugubrious Sport-Lover

Nor at his football match is Squire more gay—
Heart-rending verse describes funereal play;
While swarming adjectives in idle ranks,
As dumb spectators, load the groaning planks,
See the fat nouns, like porky forwards, sprawl
Into a scrum that never heels the ball—
A mass of moving bottoms like a sea,
All fatter than his head, if that could be;
While still attentive at their clumsy calves
The adverbs pine away, dejected halves,
The verbs hang useless by, like unfed threes
With trousers idly flapping in the breeze,
And while they strike their arm-pits for some heat
Or idly stamp their splayed trochaic feet,
The two full-backs of alternating rhyme
Walk sadly up and down to kill the time.

*

Can nothing, then, his woeful heart beguile,
No earthly pleasure soothe him to a smile?
Yes, when his editorial hands he rubs
And demonstrates this laureate of the pubs,
That 'all good poets have belonged to clubs'.
'Froth-blowing' Dantes throng into his mind
And 'Kit-Kat' Miltons, heartily inclined:
Or best of all to staunch his tearful flow—
When some great poet to the grave must go,
The parson-jackal ceases from his groans
To make his pulpit of the Lion's bones,
Then comes the simper to his drooping jaws,
Upon the royal mane he wipes his paws

And he who shed for 'Willie' his last tear
Will lift his leg for Lawrence on his bier.[1]

The Lexicon of Youth

But of all other cults that here are found,
The cult of 'Youth' most firmly holds its ground—
'Young poets' as they call them in *The Nation*
Or 'writers of the younger generation'—
Spry youths, some under ninety, I could swear,
For two had teeth and one a tuft of hair
And all a die-hard look of grim despair:
Real Peter Pans, who never age in mind,
But at the age of ninety wake to find
They've left ripe age and manhood far behind.

But to describe the rest would be a bore
Though of strange cults there were as many more:
For now the sun and moon are changing shift,
The worker stars come out into the lift
And at their windows, with the pipes alit,
Exchanging gossip with their neighbours sit,
While poor Orion, followed by his tyke,
Trudges upon his way, without a bike.

The Literary Weekend

The Stately Homes of England ope their doors
To piping Nancy-boys and crashing Bores,
Where for weekends the scavengers of letters
Convene to chew the fat about their betters—
Over the soup, Shakespeare is put in place,
Wordsworth is mangled with the sole and plaice,
And Milton's glory that once shone so clear
Now with the gravy seems to disappear,
Here Shelley with the orange peel is torn
And Byron's gored by a tame cuckold's horn.

[1] T. E. Lawrence (1888–1935), 'Lawrence of Arabia'.

By now the knives and forks are cleared away
My wanton muse, continuing the day,
Summons, from Venus' grove, a moulted dove
To Georgiana's Summer School of Love.
Like some Y.M. and W.C.A.
It welcomes waifs whom love has cast away—
A sort of Hostel where we seem to feel
The earnest pulsing of some high ideal—
'Be your own Shakespeare. Step it with the fashion.
Broadcast your love and Pelmanize your Passion.
Our short-cut to the Passions and the Arts—
A correspondence course in seven parts—
Try it! We sterilize our Cupid's darts.
Up-to-date methods: breezy situation:
And only twenty minutes from the station.
Good vegetarian catering. Worth your while!
And furnished in the "Ye Old Tea Shoppe" style:
The beds are heated up at nine precisely—
And Raymond plays the gramophone so nicely!'
Hither flock all the crowd whom love has wrecked
Of intellectuals without intellect
And sexless folk whose sexes intersect:
All who in Russell's burly frame admire
The 'lineaments of gratified desire',
And of despair have baulked the yawning precipice
By swotting up his melancholy recipes
For 'happiness'—of which he is the cook
And knows the weight, the flavour, and the look,
Just how much self-control you have to spice it with,
And the right kind of knife you ought to slice it with:
How to 'rechauffe' the stock-pot of desire
Although the devil pisses on the fire:
How much long-suffering and how much bonhomie
You must stir up, with patience and economy,
To get it right: then of this messy stew
Take the square root, and multiply by two,
And serve lukewarm, before the scum congeals,
An appetizer for your hearth-side meals.
All who have learned this grim felicity
And swotted bliss up, like the Rule of Three,
As if life were a class-examination
And there were penance in cohabitation:
All who of 'Happiness' have learned the ropes

I   129

From Bertrand Russell or from Marie Stopes,[1]
To put their knowledge into practice, some
With fierce determination dour and glum,
But all with earnest faces, hither come.

The Literary Dinner

Dinner, most ancient of the Georgian rites,
The noisy prelude of loquacious nights,
At the mere sound of whose unholy gong
The wagging tongue feels resolute and strong,
Senate of bores and parliament of fools,
Where gossip in her native empire rules;
What doleful memories the world suggests—
When I have sat like Job among the guests,
Sandwiched between two bores, a hapless prey,
Chained to my chair, and cannot get away,
Longing, without the appetite to eat,
To fill my ears, more than my mouth, with meat,
And stuff my eardrums full of fish and bread
Against the din to wad my dizzy head:
When I have watched each mouthful that they poke
Between their jaws, and praying they might choke,
Found the descending lump but cleared the way
For further anecdotes and more to say.
O Dinners! take my curse upon you all,
But literary dinners most of all,
Where I have suffered, choked with evening dress
And ogled by some frowsy poetess,
While pretty housemaids with their ankles fine,
Serving the dishes, pouring out the wine,
Seem sent on purpose with their dainty legs
To tantalize our patience to the dregs
As with loose thoughts and roving eyes astray
We strive to focus on 'the latest play'.

*

But cursed be poetesses, thin or fat,
Who give these dinners of eternal chat,

[1] Feminist and ardent advocate of birth-control; author of a widely circulated
treatise on *Married Love*. A sort of English counterpart to Margaret Sanger.

Where knife and fork dissect the latest plays
And criticism serves for mayonnaise;
Where of the Hawthornden the latest winner
Is served as joint or sirloin at the dinner,
And, succulent to busy tongues as pork,
Suffers the martyrdom of knife and fork:
Where the last novel, in a salver set,
Is masticated, à la vinaigrette,
By hungry cannibals till naught remains
Of the poor calf that wrote it, or his brains,
All his fine feelings and his tender fancies
Ruthlessly ravened by his fellow-nancies,
The fruit of all his labour sucked to strips
And nothing left of it, but peel and pips—
Cain had more Christian mercy on his brother
Than literary nancies on each other.

*

But with the coffee, Gossip hoists her sails
And over literary chat prevails:
Like summer whirlwinds, raising as they run
A cloud of dust to hide the golden sun,
Distorting even the strong arms of oaks,
So on her way the angry goddess smokes
Funnelled with roaring mouths, whose trombone blare
Scatters the legioned echoes of the air;
Through the assembled throng she rumbles past
And every brain, a feather in the blast,
And every tongue, a fluttering leaf of noise,
Surrenders to her all-commanding joys.
When sparrows loudest raise their twittering cries
We know there is a falcon in the skies:
When loudest cluck the dunghill-scratching dames
We know some eagle to the zenith flames
Casting his shadow on their farmyard games:
So when the gossips loudest squeak and cluck,
Or startled heads beneath their pinions tuck,
Look up, and see whose shadow cuts the ray
In those clear heights of intellectual day
Where eagles mate, who only stoop to slay:
Perhaps some Lewis[1], winged with laughter, soars

---

[1] Wyndham Lewis, painter, philosopher, novelist, satirical essayist; associated with Ezra Pound in the magazine *Blast*, which he edited for many years. Probably his best known work is *Time and Western Man* (1927).

And in his wake the laughing thunder roars
To see the fear he scatters as he goes
And hear the cackle of his dunghill foes—
How Ellis Roberts[2] to his perch will cling
And shamming dead, his head beneath his wing,
Though always full of literary news,
When Lewis writes, suppresses the reviews:
How this same Roberts, stuttering, explains
His bright blue funk of honesty and brains,
And trapped, repents the evil of his ways
Stampeding headlong into frantic praise:
How Nicolson[1] who in his weekly crack
Will slap the meanest scribbler on the back,
Who praises every Gertie, Bess, or Nelly,
That ever farrowed novels from her belly,
At the mere thought of Lewis goes quite blue
And to a cackle turns his weekly coo—
And so with all the weekly-scrawling crew.
Though to fight cleanly back they are not able,
They'll get their own back at the dinner-table
Where, armed with knife and fork, entrenched they sit
Encouraged more by numbers than by wit,
And by the wordy goddess urged to battle
Fight out their Bannockburns of tittle-tattle.
While truth in terror from the slaughter flies
And probability in anguish dies—
For Gossip over all our fates presides
And rules from far the literary tides,
And he who best performs her sacred rites
The goddess for his industry requites,
And to more dinners cordially invites.

The Poet as Model

Here ends my fable, just as I could wish,
And if for any moral you should fish,
You may sit trolling minnows day and night
For all I care—yet never feel a bite.

[1] Reviewer and literary dilettante; author of *Reading for Pleasure*.
[2] Harold Nicolson, diplomat, politician, historian, biographer, long-time literary columnist for the London *Spectator*.

And if you should regret the precious time
You've spent to read (as I to write) this rhyme,
Deploring that a poet thus should sink
To daubing simpletons with Stephen's ink,
Who, long before this fantasy was written,
Were blue with it as any ancient Briton,
And covered with their own from head to foot
As any grimy chimney-sweep with soot—
Remember how King David spent his leisure,
Between his deep devotions and his pleasure,
Leaving at times both muse and concubines
To hack the foreskins off the philistines—
An innocent and pleasing hobby, such
As to his fame supplies a human touch,
Endearing him as do the anecdotes
Of Alfred's cakes and Shelley's paper boats—
Such intimate and unimportant details
As Plutarch in his lives of heroes retails,
Opining as he does so that such facts
Endear as much as high, heroic acts:
And so in David's case, and so in mine—
Though foreskin-snipping was not his chief line,
Such foibles served to pass his idler hours
Without diminishing his lyric powers
And in no way detracting from his fame
And prowess in love's broncho-busting game,
Where many a lively filly he bestrode
And to the winning-post of glory rode.

*

So in all eyes I hope these lines will clear me,
And to the world in general endear me—
Especially to all dog-breeding fans,
To Septuagenarian Peter-Pans,
To Bloomsburies, to Fabians, to Sissies,
To swotters-up of philosophic blisses,
To busybodies of the wagging tongue
And all whose follies have remained unsung,
Some of whom are good fellows, I admit,
And gain in niceness what they lack in wit:
But whose collective dictatorial rule
Would wake the devil in the tamest mule—
For they're all members of the self-same school,

And drilled, like Fascists, to enforce on all
The standards of the middling and the small:
By force of numbers sure of their position
Armed, not with wit, but endless repetition,
With endless space and time to cut their capers
Whether in weekly or in daily papers,
Resolved all other causes to defy
And boost the pusillanimous on high!
So if you be so vulgar or stiff-necked
As to my Hebrew pastimes to object,
Think that in this, at least, my muse has been
Upon the side of progress and hygiene—
For doctors much to praise in it can see
And with the ancient Yiddishers agree:
And you should praise my easy moderation,
For I stop short of the wholesale castration
With which the great Anonymous would frame
Our whole identity into one same
Class, sex, community, where even name
Shall in the end be sacrificed to number,
And all distinctions in the dust shall slumber.
When by the mother on the sire begot
And quite resigned to being what-is-not,
Their fellow-ciphers shall address our sons
Not as Tom Smiths but 'Number Twenty-Ones',
When they baptize our daughters, from the score,
With indexes of Pitmanistic lore,
Not as Penelopes, Dianas, Trixies,
But 'Nine-three-double-Os' and 'Five-eight-sixes'.
When prudery, anonymity, and chat
Have killed all difference between this and that,
And progress has reformed this cosmic frame
To that great Nothing out of which it came—
The ghost and neuters who frequent that scene,
That moonlit people of the might-have-been,
Reading this page in that eventless time
Shall praise me for the meekness of my rhyme,
Who in an era of annihilation
Refrained from the wild rage of mutilation,
And gave self and identity to many
Who in their own existence hadn't any;
Singling out types from masses without name,
Which, but for my discriminating aim

Would all have seemed one genus and the same;
And from those types selecting persons too,
Who, but for me, would have remained, like you,
Dear Reader, in the world's ill-kept account,
Recurring decimals of the same amount,
Or, at the most, but very vulgar fractions
Of their respective cults, and groups, and factions;
By means of artificial respiration
Preserving Squires and Humberts for the nation
Who, much too busy to have time to think
And raking in the guineas as they clink,
Might otherwise have drowned in their own ink—
For which my muse deserves a special mention,
If not a medal, and myself a pension.

From *Flowering Rifle*

In 1935 the poet took his family to Spain, where he soon felt he had
found his spiritual homeland. In the same year he and his wife were
received into the Catholic Church, and in the proverbial way of
converts became a shade 'more Catholic than the Pope'. Campbell
loved Spain for the very reasons that had inclined so many Englishmen to despise it—the archaic economy and industrial 'backwardness',
the fierce, romantic individualism of the inhabitants, their devotion to
ancient pieties and endurance under harsh poverty, and even for the
wide prevalence of illiteracy.

The Campbells were living in Toledo during the violent disorders
that followed the triumph of the *Frente Popular* in the elections of
February 1936, and the wholesale massacres that followed the military
uprising of the following July, when, as Don Salvador de Madariaga
has put it, the mere fact of being a priest was tantamount to a capital
sentence. Campbell, who seems to have made no secret of his sym-
pathies with the insurrectionaries, found himself in some danger of
his life, and on at least one occasion was brutally beaten by some of the
Republican 'shock police' (*guardias de asalto*). Eventually he contrived
an escape with his family to the Nationalist lines, where he became a
correspondent for the London *Tablet*. According to his own account,
he took some part in the fighting with the Carlist *Requetés*, but this
has been disputed.

It may be difficult for the generation which has come to maturity since the Spanish Civil War to realize how intensely it engaged the passions of European and American intellectuals, especially after the Russian, Italian and German interventions had converted it into a conflict of international ideologies. Virtually all the well-known writers in the U.S. and in Great Britain embraced the Republican cause and became its ardent propagandists, though a few like George Orwell and John Dos Passos were subsequently sickened by the cynical treacheries of the Communists and the murderous activities of the Stalinist Tcheka against the rival parties of the Left.

The liberals viewed the struggle as one of enlightenment against reaction, of freedom against tyranny, of the oppressed against their oppressors. Campbell, like many of his new-found co-religionists, saw it primarily as one phase of the ultimate conflict of Christ and Antichrist;[1] but he saw it also as the rebellion of the free human spirit against the schemes of ideologues and doctrinaire social reformers. He had often said that though he loved men he had no patience with the abstract 'mankind', or 'humanity', in whose name the reformers presumed to speak and act. In *Flowering Rifle* he gives full rein to his hatred of utopianists, Freudians, Marxists, birth-control advocates, Anglican divines and heretics in general, as well as to his admiration of the Spanish nationalists. It is a highly prolix and carelessly written poem in which the impassioned partisan wholly submerges the satirist. Some passages, however, are still of interest.

The Contending Forces

A hundred years of strife with warring vans
Had winnowed Spain in two distinctive clans
Upon the left, inflammable, the chaff,
Corn to the right, the vulnerable half,

[1] In the Spanish field there appeared exactly the same symptoms as had appeared in Russia; massacre, arson, despotic control and the rest of it. But there was this difference, that in Spain the various forces which for very different reasons supported the national tradition and the religion thereof took the initiative before things had gone very far ... The issue has not been decided ... but ... it most certainly will not be universally decided from action in that one Spanish field alone. A universal battle has to be fought out and as it proceeds will be, like all universal battles, based on universal philosophies ... There will appear in it more and more clearly ... the division between the two spirits, utterly and essentially enemy one to the other, each working for the total extinction of the other: Christ and anti-Christ. —Hilaire Belloc, *The Crisis of Civilization*, 1937.

And thus in Spanish history began
The war between the Wowser[1] and the Man—
Him that through tortoise-shell the rainbow saw
And ate his breakfast through a dead man's jaw,
Who over lenses droops his godless lugs,
To regulate his life by those of bugs,
And whether it would better them or not,
Upon all others would impose his lot:
To figures who would subjugate our souls,
And hold a meeting when the tempest rolls,
By dead statistics would control a city
And run a battleship with a committee:
Though through the world wherever he prevailed,
His meddlesome experiments have failed:
Whether at work by the Infernal Lake,
He urge the world to war for peace's sake
Like a snug lawyer fostering the Feuds
From which his slimy livelihood exudes,
Or godless surgeon in a sinecure
Who farms the cancers he pretends to cure,
And at all costs will keep the sickness sound
With busy Mafias working underground:
But when by pulling wires and licking stamps
The nearest to his victory he ramps,
And (history can testify the rule)
Would leap into the saddle from his stool
The bronco Life, with angry snort of fire,
Has ever boomeranged four feet entire
And stamped him like a cockroach in the mire.

Upon the Right his would-be victim stood,
Armed chiefly with a sense of Bad and Good,
Who had retained erect his classic form
Through all the epidemics of Reform:
Catastrophes of progress failed to bow
His haughty gaze and heaven-seeking brow:
His mother wit rejected any movement

[1] Wowser is any kind of puritan killjoy, socialist and fabian, or pedant. There is a prophetic inkling here of the close bond between false teeth and socialism—before Bevan's 'buckshee' dentures were heard of.—R.C.

The term 'wowser'—of uncertain etymology, or none—is said to have originated in Australia towards the end of the nineteenth century. It was popularized in the United States by the late H. L. Mencken, who applied it chiefly to proponents of the prohibition laws.—Ed.

That bid him cut his throat for self-improvement,
Nor would he hack away his legs or arms
Because his sires had used them on the farms:
Whose life's a Georgic, orderly and clean,
Who long has learned what dud reformers mean,
Shrewd in philosophy the fraud to scout
In labour proud, in worship most devout,
Who reads less nonsense from his running brooks
Than waiters, primer-proud, with knowing looks,
Can mumble out of newspapers and books.

The Red Terror in Toledo

We saw the rabble, absolute in might,
Loosed from the gaols, armed from the magazines,
Turning the streets to shambles and latrines.
With weeks for Centuries, in killed and burned,
The Roman circuses to life returned,
Trebled themselves, the Caesars to depose,
And throned the Comrade with the purple nose,
Where cranium measurements became the Crown
And Finger-Prints the seal of all renown,
And the fierce spirochete, with might and main,
The raging dog-star of the human brain,
Knouting the cells, became the ruling Tsar,
To vomit fire and pestilence afar,
While syphilis and alcohol began
The death-dance of Regenerated Man,
And Christians learned, upon a stage more grand,
What bloody Circus was our Native land!

Theirs[1] were the Aegis and the thunderbolts,
That from the towering pylon loose the volts,
Where roost the rookeries of winged words,
And shake them through the sky like migrant birds
Which have the power of panic in their wings
To bear the lies to foreign states and kings:
Out-plaguing Egypt, never hummed the skies
With locusts as the ether now with lies

[1] The pronoun obviously refers not to the Christians but to the Republican government and its literary and journalistic sympathizers.

Nor Lenin's 'mightiest arm' more fiercely plied
Its Red vendetta against human pride,
Believed by most: for in its cause to plead
Negligent honour keeps no lawyer fee'd,
And Propaganda ill accords with pride
But barks its head off on the guilty side—
To set the world against us with its votes
Whose only crime was to defend our throats;
Until those towering trees, that leaved with lies,
Began to flower with answers and replies,
Like bees and humming-birds to sip the dew
The churchman and the intellectuals flew.
And never yet were trilled with livelier notes
The Tartuffades of Anglican devotes.[1]

*

But of what followed, how shall it be written?
My coward's pen over this thing would gloss
And still my fancy like a nervous kitten
Is clawing at the skein of Atropos—
Cut off from the Alcázar[2] as we lay
With nothing save to listen and to pray,
To listen and to start at fancied sounds
While the Infernal searchers went their rounds,
And life, a fly upon a rum-glass rim
Was subject to the vilest drunkard's whim,
While Death, that kind old wowser with a scythe,
That bearded skeleton with hairless poll,
Seemed but a Lansbury, cheerful and blithe,
A grand old Father Christmas of the soul,
Warm-hearted, benevolent, and kind,
Pickwick in character, Attlee in mind,
In podgy comfort Canterbury's Dean—

[1] Tartuffade: An exercise in hypocrisy. From the character in Molière's play.

[2] Hundreds of Toledans, including many women and children, had taken refuge in the ancient Alcázar on the hill overlooking the River Tagus, where about a thousand Nationalist troops, mostly Civil Guards and military cadets, commanded by Colonel Ituarte Moscardó had barricaded themselves after failing to take over the city at the beginning of the uprising. Late in July the besiegers captured Moscardó's young son Luis. The boy was put on the telephone—for some reason the lines had not been cut—to tell his father he was to be shot unless the Alcázar were immediately surrendered. 'Then, my son,' said the Colonel, 'you must die bravely.' 'Yes, papa,' was the reply. 'A big kiss. Good-bye!' Young Moscardó was killed by the Red Militia, but the Alcázar held out until Franco's forces entered the city in September.

Compared to *him* we later heard and saw
To *him* we scented in the Night obscene,
The red hyena, when the rabid froth
In stalactites was drooling from his jaw:
And heard the flesh of women torn like cloth
By female claws: and high above their screams,
Like horrors towering over madmen's dreams
To set the coldest analysts acreep,
The chuckle, and the cackle, and the laughter,
With which that shrill hyena chilled the steep
Crooning their eyeless agonies to sleep—
Most unbelievable and gloating rumour,
Abomination flawless and profound,
Loathing turned joy, as if some fearful tumour
Could find expression in the realm of sound:
Or be translated by a rabid hound,
With hoary mane erect and foetid breath,
Into a cry whose echo in the gloom
Would jog with fear the very bones of death
And bristle up the grass upon the tomb.

*

Than one such night as those of which I tell
I'd sooner have five years of Teruel:[1]
To their suspense the air raids seemed too brief
Instead of terror bringing us relief . . .
For there was little difference in one's lot
Whether set free, or whether to be shot,
For freed, it was the gauntlet of the streets,
To lurk in jakes and infamous retreats,
Nearing our quarters with increasing dread—
And some to find our families were dead:
Then without arms, only to have your knife
With which to free your children or your wife
Should the she-werewolves hit upon your spoor
Or bad luck steer them shrieking to your door.
There where we saw the Marist brothers fall
And in their smoking blood upon the wall
'So kills the Cheka' grimy fingers scrawl:
And when they held their rifles to my chest
To save my bacon with a queasy jest,

---

[1] In Southern Aragón where the Republican forces withstood a long and bloody series of attacks before it fell to the Nationalists in February 1938.

To take with gratitude their rifle butts—
My face a pulp that it might save my guts.

Desecration of the Churches

The scythe and hammer painted on the wall
Foretold the workless times that should befall,
The skull and crossbones charcoaled here and there
Were auguries of famine and despair,
Where villages already had been turned
To offal-heaps, their churches sacked or burned,
And some to stables, some to brothels turned,
Where the confessionals, as oft we find,
To rites of contraception are resigned—
For things of faith completely to destroy
Their mystic love of sacrilege would cloy,
And still, as the devoutest nuns that live,
They feed on what religion has to give.
Picture the 'Godless League' without a god
As music for their sheeny Eisteddfod!
Both atheists and godlessness would out
Had they no God to chew the fat about;
Even the Fiend, to reinforce his sprite,
And get the courage for his daily fight,
Though backwards, says his rosary every night!

And what if García Lorca died for this
Caught bending over that forlorn Abyss
For some mephitic whim his soul that spliced,
As once he boasted, with the Antichrist?
This weary Faustian hunger for the void
An age of intellectuals has destroyed;
In him another Marsyas sang and died,
The victim of the God that he defied.[1]

[1] The circumstances attending the slaying of the famous poet, Federico García Lorca, after the Nationalist seizure of Granada in August 1937, are still a matter of great mystery. Though he had many friends among Leftist writers, he had always been indifferent to politics. Some believe that he was shot by Civil Guards in revenge for the unfriendly poem he had written about them (see Campbell's translation, page 202). This is at least as tenable as Campbell's theory that he was killed because of his well-known fondness for gypsies and his alleged participation in some of their alleged sexual orgies.

It was his fate with his own age to die—
That of the fevered sin and languid eye.

On the Leftist Poets

Daring the rage of all who vainly think
Against a Nation to uphold a Stink,
In the fat snuggery of Auden, Spender,
And others of the selfsame breed and gender,
Who hold by guile the fort of English letters
Against the final triumph of their betters,
Muzzle the truth, and keep the Muse in fetters
While our own hoary sages with white hairs
Must cringe to them, like waiters on the stairs,
And few but Wyndham Lewis and myself,
Disdain salaaming for their praise and pelf,
With cleansing bombs to air the stuffy dens
Wherein they pick their noses with their pens,
Once more in naked blasphemy I stalk
And dare to prove I am not made of pork,
To flaunt this flaming heresy, the Truth,
Before the senile owl-roosts of our youth
Whom monkeys' glands seem powerless to restore,
As Birth Control was profitless before,
Which, sponsored by their mockery of a Church,
Like stranded barbels, left them in the lurch,
Whose only impact on the world's affairs
Has been to cause a boom in Rubber shares,
Who come to battle with both arms held up
And ask to be invited home to sup—
While back at home, to sound their battle-horn,
Some self-aborted pedants stray forlorn
And pity those who venture to be born.

The Virus of Literacy

Let such as Bartlett[1] blame their lack of spelling

[1] Vernon Bartlett, journalist, novelist, broadcaster on foreign affairs; editor of
the *World Review*.

For the subhuman crime he finds repelling,
Not on the damned philosophy he preaches
That mostly through the press its feeler reaches:
Do Bushmen or Bechuanas fall so low
Though on their Baobabs no primers grow?
It was the literate lounging class of Spain
That first conceived this Rabies of the brain.
The hardest workers, those that read the least,
Could still distinguish Beauty from the Beast—
The dope-fiends of cheap literature are first
To get their notions by the Kremlin cursed,
And reading without wisdom is to blame
For half the world destroyed with blood or flame—[1]
By Left-wing reading incapacitated
Either to tolerate or be tolerated.
Experience better serves the most Unread
Who carry no Boloney home to bed.

From *Talking Bronco*[2]
The Bronco's Retort

However that may be, it is a Law—
Let nobody deride the equine jaw,
For when men prove too dumb, the Gods will pass
The lowdown through the jawbone of an ass,
Or talking horse (whichever comes along)
Providing that the bone is hard and strong,
With blows, or words, that rankle twice as sore,
To cuff them into decency once more!
By tuning up that mandible of bone
Darius' stallion whinnied him a throne:
Achilles' vocal horse, and Balaam's Mule
Could put the best astrologers to school:
'Twas from a horse's kick, superb and strong,
The fountain sprang of prophecy and song:
And what is Pegasus, that mystic force,

[1] I notice that Bertrand Russell made the same statement about fifteen years after, and ten years too late. Nothing, no idea or thought is ever allowed to come out of the bag in England or U.S. until it has lost impetus or interest.—R.C.

[2] A sobriquet applied to Campbell by an irritated reviewer.

But part an aeroplane and part a horse,
And part a grand-piano for recitals
With cords and harpstrings humming in his vitals,
(While Bach and Beethoven, with angelchoirs,
Funambulize upon the strings and wires):—
A grand piano, galloping the sky,
Expert in every sphere, to sing or fly,
Or drive a tailshot in MacSpaunday's eye![1]

*

Then call me all the Horses that you like!—
You will not find such virtues in a Tyke
That follows beaten armies in the rear
Alternately beset with greed and fear
And brings bad luck to every cause he scabies
Far worse than if he'd bitten it with rabies.

Flight of the Republicans

As careful of their pockets as their skin
Except when their own 'comrades' do them in
(As happened to Durruti[2] and to Nin)[3]
They left no redder stain their faith to write
Than what they sweat or piddled in their fright
In drops as yellow as their oaths were red—
And as they've written so shall they be read,
With all who try to stutter their apology
(From Duffduff down to Spaunday's last anthology)
And all who farmed the carnage for good pay
Though from the bayonets they kept far away,
From Koestler down to Ernest Hemingway.
For see the Pasionaria[4] (with her swag)

[1] Campbell's portmanteau name for poets who had aligned themselves on the opposite side of the Spanish conflict. Evidently compounded from (Louis) MacNiece, (Stephen) Spender, (W. H.) Auden and Day (Lewis).

[2] Buenventura Durruti, Anarchist leader, slain during the siege of Madrid, probably by another Anarchist.

[3] Andrés Nin, leader of the Trotskyist POUM. Arrested by the Stalinist Tcheka and murdered in prison.

[4] Dolores Ibarruri. Fanatical and fiery Communist amazon; famous for her speeches in the Republican Cortes and over the Madrid radio; fled to France when the Casado–Miaja junta took power for the purpose of arranging a surrender and ending the war.

Escaping weeks before they struck their flag.
Preceded by a dozen fat poltroons
Each with ten dewlaps frilled in red festoons
To pose for anticlerical cartoons,
And dice for loot, in Mexican saloons.
But when the golden guineas cease to clink
And some new racket heaves the seas of ink,
The truth will out, and cry from shore to shore
When Bloomsbury and Fleet Street are no more.

The British Leftist

His leash of heads will bark, as he has shown
For every cause or country save his own.
Fortunate Country! to avert an omen
Worse than the leftwing vulture to the Roman.
For where was he, when England stood alone?
This Bogus Proletarian, the Drone
Who stood beside the Worker (*while it paid*)
Seeks every ruse his Gospel to evade
Appeals to privilege of class and wealth,
To save his pockets and preserve his health,
In ministries, where cowardice makes free,
He settles, like the vulture on the tree,
Snuffling his snout in other people's gore
As first in Spain he learned the trick before
With his ten-guinea throat-lump, gilded tear,
And Fox and Metro bringing up the rear,
Commercializing slaughter, with the Deans,
Press-Barons, Earls, Bishops, and Picture-Queens,
Who rushed headlong on Sleeping-car Safaris
And made their Klondyke of the Manzanares.
Where British Intellectuals made their pile
And Book-Clubs flourished in prodigious style,
Survey the wilderness they made of Spain
As rich in Sobstuff as devoid of grain,
As fat with tragedy as lean of meat
And full of Copy as forlorn of wheat.

Triumph of the Couplet

Free verse and prose are slippers for the dons
Unfit to clang this marching age of bronze:
The true vernacular a thorax throws
And leads the rhyme and meter by the nose;
It takes the gradients at a marching tread
Alert for all the ambushes ahead,
And when it finds some wild romantic dream
Has broken loose, with tousled hair astream,
It's easy to collect it on one's pen
As passing troops collect a wayside hen:
And many a dream poor Spaunday lives to cluck
Has ended thus, upon my bayonet stuck,
All neatly barbecued, with careless art,
To fritter on the campfire of my heart!
So you can back the couplet every time,
With its ten fingers twirling thumbs of rhyme,
To seize and clamp the trailing thoughts they fray
And scatter like tobacco by the way,
And in iambics fold them, neatly set,
As nimble fingers scroll a cigarette,
For memory to case them in his breast
And smoke at leisure, as it suits him best.

For what poor Spaunday never understands—
The couplet is a verbal pair of hands
With a two-handed punch, more clean and deft
Than his one-armed and butterfisted Left.
The stumps and bunions of our modern prose
And of free verse, will never pluck the rose,
Or lace the boot, or prime the hand-grenade
That sinks their pink Utopias in the shade,
Though flung from five years distance, in the dark,
To burst prophetic on the chosen mark.
I litter no parades with cornucopias
Of stale ice-cream, or derelict Utopias,
To lie like last week's picnic, spoil the view—
And leave one so much cleaning up to do!

THE
ARS POETICA OF
HORACE

THE *ARS POETICA* OF HORACE

This engaging translation shows Campbell's mastery of the pentameter couplet. But though the verse pattern is Augustan, the idiom is lively and colloquial, reflecting at its best the shrewdness and humour of the original.

The *Ars Poetica*—or more correctly, the scholars tell us, the *Epistle to the Pisos*, possibly the son and grandsons of Caesar's father-in-law, Lucius Calpurnius Piso Caesonius—though apparently unfinished, is one of the world's most celebrated manuals of literary instruction and long had a deep influence on European dramatic writers. The theme is how a play ought and ought not to be constructed. Horace is said to have adopted the general rules of an obscure Greek grammarian called Neoptolemus and to have appended ironic comments of his own. The *Ars Poetica* is the source of many familiar literary tags, such as

Parturient montes; nascetur ridiculus mus

for which Campbell gives us, somewhat redundantly,

'So might labour some huge hill,
Struggle in agonizing throes, and after
Bring forth a mouse deserving of our laughter.'

Much happier, however, is his rendering of

Indignor ... dormitat Homerus
'I grieve when Homer nods,'

and of

*Amphora coepit
Institui: currente rota urceus exit?*
'What was to be a wine jar will be found
A milk jug when the potter's wheel goes round.'

The Art of Poetry

(Dedicated to the Pisos, the Father and his Two Sons)

Say, were a painter to a horse's neck
To fit a human head, then fledge and fleck
With motley plumes strange limbs picked up at random,
Hitching a fine girl's body in a tandem

To a foul fish, for its posterior half—
At such a sight could you forbear to laugh?
A written book would prove as strange a fright
Believe me, my dear Pisos, as the sight
Of such a picture, were it fashioned so,
And, like a sick man's dream, so mixed, that no
Headpiece or foot could fit to any single
Whole form, but all chaotically mingle.
You say that painters with us poets share
An equal right to chance things, and to dare.
We know it. All the license that we claim
We grant to them: but not to mate what's tame
With what is fierce, to marry snakes with birds,
Or roaring tigers to the bleating herds.

Some works prance forth and promise in their stride,
Patched with fine purple, to shine far and wide
With grand beginnings—on Diana's grove
And altar: on 'the mazy streams that rove[1]
Through lush fields'; on the rainbow, or the Rhine
Painted descriptively in words as fine.
Such works are for another time, not now.
To paint a cypress one may well know how,
But what if one's commissioned, for one's cheque,
To paint a sailor swimming from a wreck[2]
That's battered by the waves beyond repair,
While hope seems lost, and life is in despair?
What was to be a wine jar will be found
A milk jug when the potter's wheel goes round.
In short, whatever work you undertake,
Simple and uniform be what you make.

Father, and both sons worthy such a sire!
Semblance is what we poets most admire.
Affecting briefness—I obscurely darkle:
Or smoothness—then I lose all verve and sparkle:
One bard grows turgid when he would seem grand:
One, fearing thunder, crawls along the sand:

[1] Apparently in this passage he is referring to, or quoting from, well-known contemporary poems, now lost.—R.C.
[2] Such works were commonly commissioned as ex-votos to hang in temples, by sailors who had escaped from wrecks. The practice continues today in Italy, Spain and Portugal.—R.C.

One who attempts too lavishly to vary
A single subject, if he is not wary,
Will make wild boars the natives of the seas
Or populate with porpoises the trees.
If to shun dangers we too wildly start,
We'll meet disaster, if we lack true art.
Near the Aemilian school, far down the Row,
There is a certain sculptor that I know,
Who moulds bronze well when doing hair or nails,
But it's with the whole body that he fails.
Now, when I want to write, I would no more
Wish to resemble him, than if I wore
My nose turned sideways, though folk thought me fine
For my black eyes and raven locks ashine.
Oh, choose a subject equal to your strength,
You poets! And consider at great length
What load your back and shoulders must refuse
And what is best adapted to your thews.
Choose but a subject well within your border
And you'll enjoy the clearness born of order:
The language will reward you with abundance
And you'll escape confusion and redundance.
If I err not, this is the grace of measure
And constitutes its excellence and pleasure—
That every thing be said at the right second,
Cancelling anything that might be reckoned
Unfit for present use, or storing it
For apter time and place, as should befit
One who attempts a poem. With due care
And taste, you'll win success; you might prepare
Some pretext to renew a well-worn word
With sound and meaning until then unheard.
Then, if perhaps some new ice must be broken
To speak abstruse new things, till now unspoken,
You'll get a splendid chance new words to coin
Unknown to Romans of the kilted loin.[1]
New words, if they're not overdone too far,
Will be accepted, if you fill your jar,
Sparingly always, from a Grecian fount.
Yet why can Plautus or Caecilius count
On Romans for the very full amount
Of license, which to Virgil and to Varius

[1] The ancient Romans wore loin cloths, not togas as in Horace's time.—R.C.

151

They now deny? My small due, though precarious,
Why should they grudge? since in the ancient tongue
Of Ennius and of Cato new terms sprung
To life. It always was, and will be, licit
That new terms for new things should be implicit,
And that new coinage should be stamped, and printed,
And dated with the year when it was minted.
As forests change their leaves at each year's end
The earliest leaves to sprout the first descend—
So it's with words: down falls the race outworn:
And like the young of human-kind, new-born,
The young words thrive and bloom. Ourselves and all
Things that are ours to death at length must fall.
We can lead Neptune far inland to shelter
Our fleets from Boreas and his stormy welter,
Or (truly royal labour!) we can dry
Marshes, where once the oars of boats were plied
But whence the neighbouring towns are now supplied
From labours of the plough: or make a river
Change course, the sprouting cornfields to deliver
Which once it flooded, but now learns the ways
To better things. Yet mortal works decay.
Still less can last the fleeting grace of speech:
Many old words, now fallen out of reach,
May be revived, and those in favour now,
If Usage wills, may wither on the bough,
For in her judgement lies the fate of all
Live speech, and by its words must stand or fall.

How deeds of Kings and Captains, and the woes
Of warfare can be sung—great Homer shows.
To distiches, the dirges of despair
Were yoked at first, and thanks for granted prayer.
Who first invented elegy, the court
Must yet decide. With his iambics (short
And long) rage armed Archilochus to smite.
Both comic sock and buskin tall unite
To find it suited to alternate talk,
And apt the cat-calls of the pit to baulk.
It fits with action too. Her lyre to grace,
The Muse reserved the Gods and all their race,
The jockey and the horse who win first place,
The champion pugilist, the loves of youth,

And praise of wine that loosens tongues with truth.
To call me poet, it would be most strange
Did I not know each symptom, beat, or change
In the verse-metres. Should I, through false shame,
Choose ignorance, rather than learned fame?

A subject fit for Comedy rebels
Against the Tragic metre. He who tells
Thyestes' tale the theme must never mock
With common speech, that suits the comic sock.
Let each theme keep the tone that is decreed.
Yet there are times when Comedy has need
Of lofty tones, as when loud Chremes storms
In swollen tones; and so the tragic norms
May vary too, as when in common prose
Peleus and Telephus recount their woes
In exiled poverty: they must discard
The thundering bombast that they spout so hard,
And in plain simple language play their part
In order thus to reach the hearer's heart.

Mere form is not enough: grace too must thrill
And lead the hearer's spirit where it will.
As most men's faces smile on those who smile,
So, too, they answer those who weep the while.
If you wish me to grieve, then you grieve first.
So, Telephus, the woes with which you're curst
Will pierce me too: but if your words suit ill,
I'll slumber on the bench, or laugh my fill.
Sad tones best suit a face expressing sorrow:
Blustering tones an angry frown should borrow:
Quips for the merry: stern words for the grave
Thus nature shapes the ways that we behave.
In meeting every change of fate she brings
Joy, or enrages us, or downward flings
And tortures us beneath a load of grief—
And then in word she makes us find relief.
If with the actor's fate his words don't fit
Guffaws will rise both from the stalls and pit.
Vast differences in their speech divide
A hero and a god: a gulf as wide
Severs a nursemaid, and a noble dame:
An old man, and a youth whose heart's aflame:

A pedlar, from a tiller of the glebe: an
Assyrian, or an Argive, from a Theban.

Follow tradition or, if you invent,
Be self-consistent. If you would present
Achilles being honoured, on the stage,
Let him be reckless, ruthless, full of rage:
Let him proclaim there are no laws for him,
Appealing to his arms with gestures grim.
Fierce let Medea be, Ixion—foresworn,
Io—a wanderer: let Orestes mourn.
If it's an untried subject you explore
With some new personage not staged before,
Let him keep constant from the first to last,
And faithful to the mould where he was cast.
To treat of humdrum things in one's own way
Is hard. And it is better, in a play,
To weave the tale of Troy into your act
Than broach an untried subject, still intact.
On public ground you will win private rights
If you don't loiter when the path invites.
Nor as a base translator word for word
Follow your model as a sheep the herd;
And if you can leap not in that narrow well
In which the billygoat of Aesop fell,
From whence for shame you never can depart
Bound by the rules of imitative art.
With such a line your poem should not start
As did the Cyclic poet's of old time—
'Of Priam's fate and famous wars I'll rhyme.'
What could this braggard give us to fulfil
His promise? So might labour some huge hill,
Struggle in agonizing throes, and, after,
Bring forth a mouse deserving of our laughter.
Better by far he is who makes no fuss
Nor strains himself, but starts his poem thus:
'Sing, Muse, about the man, who, when Troy fell,
Saw the world's customs and its towns as well.'
He does not wish to bring us smoke from fire,
But to bring light from smoke in his desire.
So that his wondrous tales may shine the best—
Of Scylla, and the Cyclops, and the rest.
Nor does he start, with Meleager's death,

Great Diomed's return: nor waste his breath
To start the siege of Troy from the twin eggs.
He rushes on, despising lees and dregs,
And hustles us towards the story's middle.
With what he can't make grand, he does not fiddle:
So cunningly does he create, so mingle
His myths and facts that in the end a single
Constancy's won—beginning, middle, ending
All in one whole harmoniously blending.

The public both expect this, and I, too,
(If sympathetic hearers you would woo,
Who'll wait the curtain and forbear to rise
Till 'Give me my applause', the singer cries)—
That you should heed the manners of each age
And suit their shifting tempers to the stage.
The child, who now can speak and walk upright,
In sporting with his playmates takes delight,
Easily flies into a rage, once in it,
Lays it aside, and changes every minute.
The beardless youth, when from his tutor freed,
Will find his chief delight in hound and steed,
And on the grassy Campus loves to roll.
As soft as wax to vice, his peevish soul
Refuses all sage counsel and control
Feckless, a spendthrift, seized with quick desires,
But quick to change them as his fancy tires.
With manhood both his character and taste
Are changed: he seeks by friends to be embraced,
And to earn wealth. A slave, now, to ambitions,
He fears the outcome of his own decisions.
An old man by great evils is beset;
Losing both health and sleep his wealth to get,
He fears to touch it, or to spend his cash.
In his affairs he lacks all fire and dash,
Procrastinates, is sparing in his hopes,
Sluggish, and dull; yet greedily he gropes
For longer life: grumbling, with surly tongue,
Praising the good old days when he was young,
And cursing modern youth. The years may bring
Many great blessings. Many too take wing
When they recede. So, lest we should assign
To youth the part of age, or else combine

155

The part of youth with manhood, let us pause
To study every age, its traits and flaws.

Deeds on the stage can either be recited
Or acted. People's minds are less excited
By things which penetrate them through the ear
Than things that to the truthful eye appear,
And what by the spectator can be seen.
Yet you must never put upon the scene
What could be done off-stage: you must not show
Anything that the audience cannot know
Through witnesses' accounts. Let not Medea
Publicly kill her sons, but in idea;
Nor impious Atreus cook his human steak,
Nor Procne turn a bird, Cadmus a snake,
In public. Were you such a trick to try,
Incredulously I would scorn the lie!

More acts, or less, than five no play should count
If it's to be encored. Let no God mount
The stage unless the knot he has to free
Is worthy the deliverer. Let there be
In conversation never more than three.

The Chorus should sustain his manly part
And function: nor between the acts depart
In what he sings from that which to his plot
Fully pertains—discarding what does not.
Siding with good, he should give counsel well,
And as a friend, striving all wrath to quell.
Encouraging the just, praising sobriety
And homely fare, with peace, and law, and piety,
He should keep secrets, and devoutly pray
Good fortune from the proud he turned away
To the unlucky persons in the play.

The wooden flute (now turned a brazen strumpet
Bound up in brass, the rival of the trumpet)
Once led the pristine chorus with its song
For seats as yet pressed by a lighter throng—
Chaste modest people, sober people, too,
Who could be counted since they were so few:

But since our victor race spread through the Earth,
And walls around its cities swelled in girth,
And since it was no longer held a crime
To pledge one's Genius in the festal time
And drink by daylight—rhythm, tune, and measure
Acquired more license, liberty, and leisure.
What good taste could be hoped for from a crowd
Which mixes boors with burghers, poor with proud,
And some still sweating from the fields they ploughed?
Since then, to the older art the flautist added
Display and pomp, as to and fro he gadded
From wing to wing, parading up and down
The sumptuous train of his pretentious gown,
Flaunting his finery, and nimbly prancing
To supplement his music with his dancing.
So, also, to the plain old fashioned lyre
Were added extra strings of twangling wire
A strange, audacious diction to inspire:
The chorus then began to utter grave
Good counsels, or with prophecies to rave
Like those of Delphi's priestess in her cave.

The bard who first in Tragedy[1] competed
For a mere paltry billygoat that bleated,
Brought naked satyrs on the stage who cracked
Lewd jests, but left the gravity intact,
For the spectators had observed the rite
Of copious libations and were tight,
And lawlessly inclined. Thus it was needful
With quips and novelties to keep them heedful.
So it behoved the poet to seek favour
Through these coarse satyrs and their goatish savour,
Before he passed to other subjects, graver.
But while we graft our jests to graver thought,
No god nor hero ever should be caught,
Redhanded, in some lowdown tavern-hovel
Using the vulgar tongue, with words that grovel.
Yet, shunning baseness, do not let your speech
Spurn the firm earth, for empty clouds to reach.
True Tragedy, scorning to speak what's trivial,

[1] Tragedy gets its name from the goat that was given as a prize to the winner
of the earliest Olympic contests between poets. It means 'goat-poetry', from *tragos*
(a goat) and *aeidō* (to sing or recite).—R.C.

(Like a proud matron forced, on the convivial
Occasion of a holy day, to dance)
Amongst the frisking satyrs looks askance.
My Piso friends, true Tragedy to write,
I'll use no trivial words my theme to slight,
Nor of what's tragic so far lose the sight
That it's no matter whether Davus speak
With Pythias, the vile and shameless Greek,
Who, cheating Simo, earned a tidy wad,
Or with Silenus, guardian of the god.
My aim is song, drawn from what's so familiar
That all who think it easy, will prove sillier,
In the attempt, than they expect. When much
Sweat has been spent, they'll fail the magic touch.
Such is the power of making terms cohere,
That beauty from the commonplace, by sheer
Sense of arrangement, shines out bright and clear.

Fauns, from the forest brought, may well beware
Of acting as if on the Public Square,
Or aping precious dandies of the city,
Or cracking jokes more crapulous than witty,
Since Roman Knights and Freemen scorn such scenes
As please the eaters of the nuts and beans.[1]
That beat, wherein a short precedes a long
Syllable's what we call Iambic song,
Which means 'fleet-footed'. It is so much fleeter
Than sense, that we miscall it the 'three-metre',
The whole line's sum perfected in their halves;
Whole legs find alibis in thighs and calves;
'Three-beats' we call it, though its beats are six,
And roll on evenly, and do not mix.
Not long ago, to give it poise and weight,
Iambus took the Spondee in its gait,
But never in the fourth foot or the second
Of the Iambus is the Spondee reckoned.
In the trimetres Accius wrote—it's rare:
And in what Ennius, without skill or care,
Unloaded on the stage—you'll find it there,
Either that in revising he'd no part,
Or that he was too ignorant of art.

[1] Those who occupied the cheap seats regaled themselves with roasted beans and chestnuts.—R.C.

158

Not every critic spots the faulty fool,
So undeserved indulgence is the rule.
But if I then stampede and jump the fence,
To a safe pardon can I make pretence?
At best, I'll have escaped without due blame,
And yet can make no bid for learned fame.
For you, Greek models are the best to handle
Whether by day, or by the midnight candle.
And yet you say 'twas our forebears who taught us
To praise the metres and the wit of Plautus . . .
Too tolerant they were—too kindly foolish
Mistaking for true wit what's coarse and mulish,
Since we by ear and finger can sort out
What's clumsy from what's right, beyond all doubt.

Thespis, they say, discovered first the Muse
Of tragedy, before her name made news.
He used to cart his plays around in wagons
Acted by clowns stained with the lees of flagons.
Aeschylus, later, improvised the planks,
Tall buskins, robes, the players' masks, and (thanks
To him) the stately gait and lofty strain
That till his time no drama could attain.
To this succeeded the old Comedy.
It won some honour, but was far too free;
Licentious to excess, it was thereafter
Checked by the law, for its injurious laughter.
The law was passed. The chorus then became
Harmlessly dumb, to its enduring shame.

Our own bards tried all styles, nor has less glory
Been won, when keeping to their native story
(Whether in tragic or in comic vein)
They cease to follow in the Grecian train.
If all our poets polished up their style
And had the patience both to pare and file,
Then Latin might have shone supreme in verse
As in armed glory, through the universe.
You then, of Numa's stock,[1] should ban all lines
Which the bard neither alters nor refines,
With many a blot, through many a lengthy day,
And polishes and files the best he may,

---

[1] The Pisos were aristocrats claiming descent from Numa Pompilius and related
to Julius Caesar's wife Calpurnia.—R.C.

Till manicured and burnished twenty times,
A well-cut nail may test and prove his rhymes.

Because Democritus says native wit
Is greater then mere art, and won't admit
Some bards to Helicon—some sprout long hair
With shaggy beards, and nails they never pare.
Shunning mankind they stray in lonely paths
And shun alike the barbers and the baths.
Thinking to join the poets' deathless ranks
If from Licinus'[1] shears he saves the hanks
Of a shag pate, that not all the hellebore
Of all three Anticyras[2] could restore.
How daft of me to purge myself of bile
Whenever lusty Spring begins to smile!
None could sing better, but it's not worth while,
I'll be the whetstone that can sharpen steel:
Although it cannot cut, I shall reveal
The poet's duties and his task: and whence
He draws his ammunition and his rations;
What nourishes him best, I'll show: what fashions
His talent: what befits him best and what
Doesn't: which course to follow, and which not.

Of all good writing wisdom is the fount.
The wise Socratic pages can recount
Your subject. When you have the theme, the words
Will follow it along in flocks and herds.
Learn what you owe your country and your friend
What love upon a parent should attend,
A guest, or brother. Learn what is expected
Of senator or judge: how war's directed
By a supreme commander in the field—
That each in his true role may be revealed.
He, who in imitative skill rejoices,
From life and manners should take living voices.
Though fashioned without grace or strength, a play
Is far more pleasing if it can display
Characters drawn to life, and has some witty

[1] Apparently a fashionable hairdresser in Rome.—R.C.
[2] Hellebore was supposed to be a cure for lunacy. The Anticyras were cities of the same name situated on a mountain range north of Corinth, where hellebore grew in great abundance. Hellebore is also a purge for bile.—R.C.

Patches of dialogue—than all the pretty,
Far-better-written verse that's void of thought,
And sounding bombast signifying naught.

The Muse gave native wit to Grecian folk:
With a rotundity of style they spoke
Lusting for fame. But we in long division,
Addition, and subtraction, learn precision,
And how to split the As[1] up into parts.
For sums and figures, we neglect the arts.
The Master says 'Now, you, Albinus' son,
Answer. If from five-twelfths the weight of one
Ounce is subtracted, what have we got left?'
A third.' 'Good! in your Business you'll be deft.
And if I add an ounce, what then?' 'A half.'
When this base passion for the Golden Calf,
This eating rust, has fouled the Roman mind,
What poetry can we expect to find
Worthy with oil of cedar to be swept
Or within boards of cypress to be kept?
Poets wish either to instruct or please
Or both at once. But do it by degrees,
And do it briefly, if you would instruct,
So that the mind retains the fruit it plucked.
One word too much will overflow and spill
After the brimming mind has had its fill,
From fancied fictions most delight is won
When nearest to reality they run.
In plays be circumspect with the unreal
Nor from the Lamia let her human meal
Be saved out of her guts—a living child.
Plays without moral purpose are exiled
From the stage by our elders. Men of race
And breeding scorn a poem without grace.
You'll win, if you mix benefit with pleasure
Teaching and charming in an equal measure.
Such is the volume by the sale of which
Publishers like the *Soscii* grow rich.
Such is the book that makes the author's name
Cross seas and centuries with lasting fame.

[1] As is a Roman bronze coin, originally weighing about a pound, reduced finally
to half an ounce.—R.C.

Yet there are errors which we can forgive
Gladly. A harpstring will not always give
The note that hand and heart wished from the harp,
And for a flat note sometimes gives a sharp.
Nor will a bow hit whatsoever prey
It aims at. But when beauties oversway
The blemishes that carelessness let fall,
Or that our nature can't prevent at all,
I will not ban such poetry. What then?
A clerk who, making copies with his pen,
Though often warned, continues still to make,
In spite of everything, the same mistake,
Merits no mercy. So the zither-twanger
Who on the selfsame string bungles with clangour
Repeatedly, is laughted at. Thus I class
The poet who so blunders, as an ass,
With Choerilus, in whom a few good lines
The more provoke our laughter, when he shines.
I grieve when Homer nods: but every song
Is liable to tedium, if long.

A poem, like a picture, may appear
Better, far off: or better, standing near.
One woos the shade: another woos the light
And challenges the critic's piercing sight.
One having pleased us once, we can admire
No more: yet of another cannot tire.
You, elder son, though wise yourself and taught
By a wise father to judicious thought,
Mark well my words (in this I am no joker)
Only in some fields can the mediocre
Be suffered. Lawyers of a middling sort
Though of the great Messala falling short,
And knowing less than Aulus, have their use,
But for a middling poet? No excuse!
Nor Gods, nor men, nor publishers permit,
Even in their wildest dreams, the thought of it!
As at a pleasant feast we take offence
At a band out of tune, unguent too dense,
Or, in Sardinian honey, poppy seed—
Since of the like the banquet had no need—
So poems, written for the souls' delight;
If they should fail to reach the sheerest height,

Fall headlong down. The man who's weak at sport
Will never to the playing field resort:
If he's bad as a bowler and a quoiter
Around the Campus he's ashamed to loiter
For dread of people's laughter and contempt.
Yet those who can't write verses still attempt
To do so, and with neither dread nor shame
Insist on interfering in the game.
Why not? He's a free man perhaps free-born
With a knight's fortune—so he's safe from scorn.

But you, my friend, will not presume to slight
Minerva's will—your judgement is so right,
So sound your sense. But if you should be tempted
To rhyme, show first the work you have attempted
To some strict Maecius: after that, deposit
The script for nine years in your father's closet.
Unpublished work, one can delete or burn.
The voice, sent forth, can nevermore return.

When men lived in the wilds, Orpheus, the prophet,
Saw their bloodthirsty life, and warned them off it,
For doing which he won the mythic fame
Of making lions and fierce tigers tame:
And of Amphion's building Thebes they tell
Like tales. His lyre moved boulders with its spell,
And led them where he wanted them as well.
Of old it was thought wise to draw a line
'Twixt private things and public: to define
The sacred from the vulgar: to keep strict
The marriage law: loose love to interdict.
To build towns, and carve laws on slabs of wood
In those old times it was considered good.
And so on poets fame and glory fell,
And deified them, and their songs as well.
Then Homer won renown. Tyrtaeus drove
Men's souls, when in the Wars of Mars they strove.
Oracles spoke in song and showed the way
To better life. The poets in their day
Could sing preferment from the hearts of kings,
And after toil, in the Pierian springs,
Delight was found. So do not blush to follow
The lyre-skilled Muse and the divine Apollo.

Concerning a good poem, men enquire
Whether from art it stems, or native fire.
I find all effort vain which sets apart
Genius from toil, nature from conscious art.
For nature's talent needs the help of science
And vice versa—both in fond alliance.
He who would win the race before the rest
Must, even as a child, have stood the test
Of heat, cold, and fatigue. He must abstain
From Venus and from Bacchus. He who blows
The oboe at the Games learned what he knows
From a feared tutor by the dint of blows.
Not so verse-writers of the present day
'My verse is wonderful,' is what they say,
'He who comes last be damned. I've but one shame
And that's to be surpassed: but all the same
I never learned a thing about the game.'
Just like the public criers who collect
Crowds for some public sale which they expect,
The poet, if he owns a rich estate
Or leases property at a high rate,
Collects his flatterers, as meat does flies,
By flashing golden bribes before their eyes.
But if his power to such a pitch extends
That he to sumptuous feasts can treat his friends,
Or stands as surety for a poor man's debt,
Or rescue one whom law-suits have beset—
Confounding interests—he will never know
Whether his friends are hypocrites or no:
And you, yourself, if wishing to be pleasant,
You purpose giving anyone a present,
For heaven's sake, while he with joys is smitten,
Don't read him any verses you have written!
For he'll cry out 'Fine! Wondrous! Perfect! Splendid!'
And beating time until the verse is ended
Grow pale, and weep with dewy eyes distended.
As you may see in funeral processions,
The hired mourners, more than the relations,
Whose grief is real, howl, rave, and tear their locks,
The flatterer, too, though in his heart he mocks,
More than the true admirer shows delight,
Rejoices, and applauds with all his might.

When monarchs wish true friendship to divine,
They put the person to the test of wine.
If you write verse, yet wish true friends to win,
Beware what lurks beneath the fox's skin.
When people read their verses to Quintilius,
His answer was straightforwardly punctilious—
'Mend this, I beg you. Then mend this': and when
You had tried vainly three or four times, then
He'd tell you to wipe everything away,
And start once more on what you had to say.
If you preferred your fluff to mending it,
He said no word: he did not mind a whit:
Without demur, he let you go your way
To be your own self-loving non-pareil.
A wise and honest judge will criticize
Limp verse in which no art or cunning lies:
Cancel what's harsh and rugged with a stroke:
Suppress pretentious bombast with a joke:
And make you light the gloom if you grow dark.
The necessary changes he'll remark—
In short he will become an Aristarch.
He will not say, 'Why hurt a friend for trifles?'
Which later may be turned on him like rifles
And wound him mortally, when once the crowd
Jeers him to scorn, and hisses him aloud.

One fears and shuns the wretch with rabies bitten,
With jaundice or fanaticism smitten,
Or by Diana's wrath made lunatic;
So men shun crazy poets like Old Nick.
Children torment them, risking kicks and blows,
But high in air the poet rears his nose
And whinnies forth his verses as he goes.
If, one day, like a birdcatcher he fell,
Star-gazing after blackbirds, in a well—
And yelled 'Help! Citizens!'—they'd let him yell!
To those who wished to save him, I would say
'Why, don't you know, he did himself away
On purpose and does not want any succours.'
And then I'd tell the story to the suckers
Of the Sicilian bard—and how he died.
Empedocles wished to be deified
In people's minds, and so he leaped inside

Erupting Etna, with cool calculation.
Poets have rights to such self-immolation.
To rescue one against his will is wrong,
When he's committing suicide in song.
To rescue him's a crime. Such if you save—
He will not cease a famous death to crave,
Nor yet consent as human to behave.
It puzzles me how he conceived this passion
To scribble in so desperate a fashion.
What's certain is, he's mad, and, like a bear
Who's burst his cage, and, roaring here and there,
With hideous din, drives crowds before his blether,
Both ignorant and learnèd, hell-for-leather.
If some poor devil falls into his grip
He hugs him to his heart and then lets rip
And will not cease till death. So leeches suck
And, till they're gorged, will never come unstuck.

TRANSLATIONS FROM THE FRENCH, SPANISH AND PORTUGUESE

———————

FROM THE FRENCH

CHARLES BAUDELAIRE
1821–67
From *Les Fleurs du Mal*

To the Reader

Folly and error, avarice and vice,
Employ our souls and waste our bodies' force.
As mangy beggars incubate their lice,
We nourish our innocuous remorse.

Our sins are stubborn, craven our repentance.
For our weak vows we ask excessive prices.
Trusting our tears will wash away the sentence,
We sneak off where the muddy road entices.

Cradled in evil, that Thrice-Great Magician,
The Devil, rocks our souls, that can't resist;
And the rich metal of our own volition
Is vapourized by that sage alchemist.

The Devil pulls the strings by which we're worked:
By all revolting objects lured, we slink
Hellwards; each day down one more step we're jerked
Feeling no horror, through the shades that stink.

Just as a lustful pauper bites and kisses
The scarred and shrivelled breast of an old whore,
We steal, along the roadside, furtive blisses,
Squeezing them, like stale oranges, for more.

Packed tight, like hives of maggots, thickly seething,
Within our brains a host of demons surges.
Deep down into our lungs at every breathing,
Death flows, an unseen river, moaning dirges.

If rape or arson, poison, or the knife
Has wove no pleasing patterns in the stuff
Of this drab canvas we accept as life—
It is because we are not bold enough!

Amongst the jackals, leopards, mongrels, apes,
Snakes, scorpions, vultures, that with hellish din,
Squeal, roar, writhe, gambol, crawl, with monstrous shapes,
In each man's foul menagerie of sin—

There's one more damned than all. He never gambols,
Nor crawls, nor roars, but, from the rest withdrawn,
Gladly of this whole earth would make a shambles
And swallow up existence with a yawn . . .

Boredom! He smokes his hookah, while he dreams
Of gibbets, weeping tears he cannot smother.
You know this dainty monster, too, it seems—
Hypocrite reader!—You!—My twin!—My brother!

The Cat

I

A fine strong gentle cat is prowling
As in his bedroom, in my brain:
So soft his voice, so smooth its strain,
That you can scarcely hear him miowling.

But should he venture to complain
Or scold, the voice is rich and deep:
And thus he manages to keep
The charm of his untroubled reign.

This voice, which seems to pearl and filter
Through my soul's inmost shady nook,
Fills me with poems, like a book,
And fortifies me, like a philtre.

His voice can cure the direst pain
And it contains the rarest raptures.
The deepest meanings, which it captures,
It needs no language to explain.

There is no bow that can so sweep
That perfect instrument, my heart:
Or make more sumptuous music start
From its most vibrant chord and deep,

Than can the voice of this strange elf,
This cat, bewitching and seraphic,
Subtly harmonious in his traffic
With all things else, and with himself.

II

So sweet a perfume seems to swim
Out of his fur both brown and bright,
I nearly was embalmed one night
From (only once) caressing him.

Familiar Lar of where I stay,
He rules, presides, inspires and teaches
All things to which his empire reaches.
Perhaps he is a god, or fay.

When to a cherished cat my gaze
Is magnet-drawn and then returns
Back to itself, it there discerns,
With strange excitement and amaze,

Deep down in my own self, the rays
Of living opals, torch-like gleams
And pallid fire of eyes, it seems,
That fixedly return my gaze.

The Red-haired Beggar Girl

White girl with flame-red hair,
Whose garments, here and there,
Give poverty to view,
    And beauty too.

To me, poor puny poet,
Your body, as you show it,
With freckles on your arms,
    Has yet its charms.

You wear with prouder mien
Than in Romance a queen
Her velvet buskins could—
    Your clogs of wood.

In place of tatters short
Let some rich robe of court
Swirl with its silken wheels
    After your heels:

In place of stockings holed
A dagger made of gold,
To light the lecher's eye,
    Flash on your thigh:

Let ribbons slip their bows
And for our sins disclose
A breast whose radiance vies
    Even with your eyes.

To show them further charms
Let them implore your arms,
And these, rebuking, humble
    Fingers that fumble

With proffered pearls aglow
And sonnets of Belleau,
Which, fettered by your beauty,
    They yield in duty.

Riffraff of scullion-rhymers
Would dedicate their primers
Under the stairs to view
    Only your shoe.

Each page-boy lucky starred,
Each marquis, each Ronsard
Would hang about your bower
    To while an hour.

You'd count, among your blisses,
Than lilies far more kisses,
And boast, among your flames,
    Some royal names.

Yet now your beauty begs
For scraps on floors, and dregs
Else destined to the gutter.
    As bread and butter.

You eye, with longing tense,
Cheap gauds for thirty cents,
Which, pardon me, these days
    I cannot raise.

No scent, or pearl, or stone,
But nothing save your own
Thin nudity for dower,
    Pass on, my flower!

Sorrow of the Moon

More drowsy dreams the moon tonight. She rests
Like a proud beauty on heaped cushions pressing,
With light and absent-minded touch caressing,
Before she sleeps, the contour of her breasts.

On satin-shimmering, downy avalanches
She dies from swoon to swoon in languid change,
And lets her eyes on snowy vision range
That in the azure rise like flowering branches.

173

When sometimes to this earth her languor calm
Lets streak a stealthy tear, a pious poet,
The enemy of sleep, in his cupped palm,

Takes this pale tear, of liquid opal spun
With rainbow lights, deep in his heart to stow it
Far from the staring eyeballs of the Sun.

The Albatross

Sometimes for sport the men of loafing crews
Snare the great albatrosses of the deep,
The indolent companions of their cruise
As through the bitter vastitudes they sweep.

Scarce have they fished aboard these airy kings
When helpless on such unaccustomed floors,
They piteously droop their huge white wings
And trail them at their sides like drifting oars.

How comical, how ugly, and how meek
Appears this soarer of celestial snows!
One, with his pipe, teases the golden beak,
One, limping, mocks the cripple as he goes.

The Poet, like this monarch of the clouds,
Despising archers, rides the storm elate.
But, stranded on the earth to jeering crowds,
The great wings of the giant baulk his gait.

Ill Luck

So huge a burden to support
Your courage, Sisyphus, would ask;
Well though my heart attacks its task,
Yet Art is long and Time is short.

Far from the famed memorial arch
Towards a lonely grave I come.
My heart in its funereal march
Goes beating like a muffled drum.[1]

—Yet many a gem lies hidden still
Of whom no pick-axe, spade, or drill
The lonely secrecy invades;

And many a flower, to heal regret,
Pours forth its fragrant secret yet
Amidst the solitary shades.

The Giantess

Of old when Nature, in her verve defiant,
Conceived each day some birth of monstrous mien,
I would have lived near some young female giant
Like a voluptuous cat beside a queen;

To see her body flowering with her soul
Freely develop in her mighty games,
And in the mists that through her gaze would roll
Guess that her heart was hatching sombre flames;

To roam her mighty contours as I please,
Ramp on the cliff of her tremendous knees,
And in the solstice, when the suns that kill

Make her stretch out across the land and rest,
To sleep beneath the shadow of her breast
Like a hushed village underneath a hill.

[1] See note to 'The Festivals of Flight', page 15.

The Dance of Death

(To Ernest Christophe)

Proud, as a living person, of her height,
Her scarf and gloves and huge bouquet of roses,
She shows such nonchalance and ease as might
A thin coquette excessive in her poses.

Who, at a ball, has seen a form so slim?
Her sumptuous skirts extravagantly shower
To a dry foot that, exquisitely trim,
Her footwear pinches, dainty as a flower.

The frills that rub her collarbone, and feel,
Like a lascivious rill against a rock,
The charms she is so anxious to conceal,
Defend them, too, from ridicule and mock.

Her eyes are forms of emptiness and shade.
Her skull, with flowers so deftly decked about,
Upon her dainty vertebrae is swayed.
O what a charm when nullity tricks out!

'Caricature', some might opine, but wrongly,
Whose hearts, too drunk with flesh that runs to waste,
Ignore the grace of what upholds so strongly.
Tall skeleton, you match my dearest taste!

Come you to trouble with your strong grimace,
The feast of life? Or has some old desire
Rowelled your living carcase from its place
And sent you, credulous, to feed its fire?

With tunes of fiddles and the flames of candles,
Hope you to chase the nightmare far apart,
Or with a flood of orgies, feasts, and scandals
To quench the hell that's lighted in your heart?

Exhaustless well of follies and of faults,
Of the old woe the alembic and the urn,
Around your trellised ribs, in new assaults,
I see the insatiable serpent turn.

I fear your coquetry's not worth the strain,
The prize not worth the effort you prolong.
Could mortal hearts your railleries explain?
The joys of horror only charm the strong.

The pits of your dark eyes dread fancies breathe,
And vertigo. Among the dancers prudent,
Hope not your sixteen pairs of smiling teeth
Will ever find a contemplative student.

Yet who's not squeezed a skeleton with passion?
Nor ravened with his kisses on the meat
Of charnels. What of costume, scent, or fashion?
The man who feigns disgust, betrays conceit.

O noseless geisha, unresisted gouge!
Tell these fastidious feigners, from your husk—
'Proud fondling fools, in spite of talk and rouge,
You smell of death. Anatomies of musk,

Withered Antinouses, beaux of dunder,
Corpses in varnish, Lovelaces of bone,
The dance of death, with universal thunder,
Is whirling you to places yet unknown!

From Seine to Ganges frolicking about,
You see not, through a black hole in the ceiling,
Like a great blunderbus, with funnelled snout,
The Angel's trumpet, on the point of pealing.

In every clime, Death studies your devicer
And vain contortions, laughable Humanity,
And oft, like you, perfumes herself with spices
Mixing her irony with your insanity!'

The Cask of Hate

The Cask of the pale Danaïds is Hate.
Vainly Revenge, with red strong arms employed,
Precipitates her buckets, in a spate
Of blood and tears, to feed the empty void.

The Fiend bores secret holes to these abysms
By which a thousand years of sweat and strain
Escape, though she'd revive their organisms
In order just to bleed them once again.

Hate is a drunkard in a tavern staying,
Who feels his thirst born of its very cure,
Like Lerna's hydra, multiplied by slaying.

Gay drinkers of their conqueror are sure,
And Hate is doomed to a sad fate, unable
Ever to fall and snore beneath the table.

The Balcony

Mother of memories, queen of paramours,
Yourself are all my pleasures, all my duty;
You will recall caresses that were yours
And fireside evenings in their warmth and beauty.
Mother of memories, queen of paramours.

On eves illumined by the light of coal,
The balcony beneath a rose-veiled sky,
Your breast how soft! Your heart how good and whole!
We spoke eternal things that cannot die—
On eves illumined by the light of coal!

How splendid sets the sun of a warm evening!
How deep is space! the heart how full of power!
When, queen of the adored, towards you leaning,
I breathed the perfume of your blood in flower.
How splendid sets the sun of a warm evening!

The evening like an alcove seemed to thicken,
And as my eyes astrologized your own,
Drinking your breath, I felt sweet poisons quicken,
And in my hands your feet slept still as stone.
The evening like an alcove seemed to thicken.

I know how to resuscitate dead minutes.
I see my past, its face hid in your knees.

How can I seek your languorous charm save in its
Own source, your heart and body formed to please.
I know how to resuscitate dead minutes.

These vows, these perfumes, and these countless kisses,
Reborn from gulfs that we could never sound,
Will they, like suns, once bathed in those abysses,
Rejuvenated from the deep, rebound—
These vows, these perfumes, and these countless kisses?

Her Hair

O fleece that down her nape rolls, plume on plume!
O curls! O scent of nonchalance and ease!
What ecstasy! To populate this room
With memories it harbours in its gloom,
I'd shake it like a banner on the breeze.

Hot Africa and languid Asia play
(An absent world, defunct, and far away)
Within that scented forest, dark and dim.
As other souls on waves of music swim,
Mine on its perfume sails, as on the spray.

I'll journey there, where man and sap-filled tree
Swoon in hot light for hours. Be you my sea,
Strong tresses! Be the breakers and the gales
That waft me. Your black river holds, for me,
A dream of masts and rowers, flames and sails.

A port, resounding there, my soul delivers
With long deep draughts of perfumes, scent, and clamour,
Where ships, that glide through gold and purple rivers,
Fling wide their vast arms to embrace the glamour
Of skies wherein the heat forever quivers.

I'll plunge my head in it, half drunk with pleasure—
In this black ocean that engulfs her form.
My soul, caressed with wavelets there may measure
Infinite rockings in embalmèd leisure,
Creative idleness that fears no storm!

Blue tresses, like a shadow-stretching tent,
You shed the blue of heavens round and far.
Along its downy fringes as I went
I reeled half-drunken to confuse the scent
Of oil of coconuts, with musk and tar.

My hand forever in your mane so dense,
Rubies and pearls and sapphires there will sow,
That you to my desire be never slow—
Oasis of my dreams, and gourd from whence
Deep draughted wines of memory will flow.

Meditation

Be good, my Sorrow: hush now: settle down.
You sighed for dusk, and now it comes: look there!
A denser atmosphere obscures the town,
To some restoring peace, to others care.

While the lewd multitude, like hungry beasts,
By pleasure scourged (no thug so fierce as he!)
Go forth to seek remorse among their feasts—
Come, take my hand; escape from them with me.

From balconies of sky, around us yet,
Lean the dead years in fashions that have ceased.
Out of the depth of waters smiles Regret.

The sun sinks moribund beneath an arch,
And like a long shroud rustling from the East,
Hark, Love, the gentle Night is on the march.

ARTHUR RIMBAUD
1854–91

Drunken Boat

I felt no more the guidance of my tow-men
As I came down by listless river-coasts.
To serve for targets, whooping Redskin bowmen
Had pinned them naked to their coloured posts.

Bearer of Flemish corn or English cotton,
I cared no more for crews of any kind.
When with my own the scuffle was forgotten,
The rivers let me rove as I inclined.

Into the furious chopping of the tides
Last winter, heedless as a child, I glided;
Nor have the unmoored headlands on their sides
Sustained so proud a buffeting as I did.

The Storm has blessed my watches in the spray:
Cork-light I danced the waves for ten whole nights
(Those everlasting maulers of their prey!)
Nor missed the foolish blink of harbour-lights.

Sweet, as to children the tart flesh of apples,
Green water pierced my shell with juicy shudder,
Spewing a wine of azure blots and dapples
That rinsed me round, dispersing helm and rudder.

Since then I have gone bathing in the hymn
Of a sea sprayed with stars and whitely creaming:
Devouring the green depths where, flotsam dim,
Sometimes a drowning man descends half-dreaming:

Where with slow-pulsing and delirious fires,
To flush the blue, while day blazed white above,
Stronger than wine and vaster than your lyres,
Ferments the crimson bitterness of love.

I've known the surf, the waterspouts, the tide:
Lightning-split skies: the dusk: the dawn upheld
Like a whole swarm of doves; and I have spied
Sometimes, what Man believes he has beheld.

Lighting long wisps in violent panoramas,
I have seen mystic horrors scrawl the sun:
Far waves, like actors in the ancient dramas,
Unroll their flickering shutters as they run.

I've dreamed the green night lit with dazzling frost
A kiss that to the sea's eyes slowly grew,
The flow of saps to human knowledge lost,
And singing phosphorescence gold and blue.

Like mad stampedes of cattle on the prairies,
With breakers I have charged the reefs and screes
For months: nor dreamed the lit feet of the Maries
Could force a snaffle of those snorting seas.

Blurring with flowers the eyes of human leopards,
I've whirled Floridas none yet set eyes on,
Where, stretching coloured reins, the Iris shepherds
Her glaucous flocks beneath the sea's horizon.

I've seen the swamps ferment, huge creels of rushes,
Where rots a whole Leviathan as it sleeps,
Amidst dead calms collapsing water-gushes,
And distances cascading to the deeps:

Glaciers, white suns, pearl waves, skies of red coals:
At limits of brown gulfs, foul objects stranded:
Where huge bug-eaten snakes from twisted boles
Fell dying with black perfumes where they landed.

I would have shown those bream of the blue billow
To children, those gold fish, those fish that sing;
Foam flowers for my escape have smoothed a pillow
And winds ineffable have waved my wing.

Tired martyr, round the poles and tropics rolled,
The wave, whose sobs my cradle rocked at ease,

Raised flowers of shade with spiracles of gold
And left me like a woman on her knees.

Half-island, tilting at my sides the frays
And tail-shots of the blond-eyed birds that scream,
I wandered, while across my flimsy stays
Drowned men descended backwards down to dream.

Lost in the hair of coves or like a shaft
Shot into birdless ether, I, lost boat,
Whose sea-drunk corpse no Hanseatic craft
Nor monitor could salvage or refloat,

Free, smoking, by the violet fog embraced,
Have broached the sky's red wall and bored it through,
Which bears, so dainty to good poets' taste,
Lichens of sun, and mucus of the blue.

Scribbled with small electric moons, mad plank,
With black sea-horses harnessed to my gunnels,
I've run, while Summer basked to dust, and sank
The jet-blue sky to swirl down blazing funnels,

I who have quaked to hear, at fifty leagues,
The rut of Behemoths and Maelstroms roar,
Threader of endless calms whom naught fatigues,
Am sick for Europe's towers of ancient lore.

Starred archipelagoes I've seen and islands
Where maddening skies, to tempt the rover, flower,
Where hide you in those nights of topless silence
(Millions of golden birds!) predestined Power?

But, true, I've wept too much. The dawns are fearful.
Each moon is loathsome. Suns are sour to me.
Salt love has bloated me and sogged me tearful.
May my keel splinter! Give me to the sea!

If there's a northern water that I crave,
It's the black slush, at scented close of day,
Whereon a child releases, sadly grave,
A boat frail as the butterflies of May.

No more, bathed in your languor, waves! I'll trim
Her seawake where the cotton-clipper flies:
Nor cross the pomp of flags and flames: nor swim
Beneath the convict-hulks' resentful eyes.

PAUL VALERY
1871–1944
The Bee

However sharp and dire you shoot
Your dart, O golden bee, I place
Only the flimsiest veil of lace
Over my frail of tender fruit.

Sting on the breast this gourd so fresh
Where love, in death or sleep, lies leaden;
So may some inkling of me redden
The rounded and rebellious flesh.

I need quick pain, a prompt alert:
Far better than a lingering hurt
The keenest pang that soonest flies.

Gold spar, light up the sense you pierce,
Infinitesimal yet fierce,
Without whose sting love sleeps or dies.

GUILLAUME APOLLINAIRE
(Guillaume Apollinaire de Kostrowitsky)
1880–1918
Sorrow of a Star

A fine Minerva of my head was daughter,
A star of blood forever marks the place
(Heaven above, and reason at the base)
Where long she had been arming for the slaughter.

That's why of all the griefs with which I'm ridden
This starred, nigh-fatal wound is not my worst.
I have a secret evil more accurst
Than any other soul has ever hidden.

And so I burn, with anguish for my pyre,
As glow-worms panting in their own hot sheen;
As in one soldier's heart all France is seen,
Or lily's heart—it's pollen-scented fire.

FROM THE SPANISH

SAN JUAN DE LA CRUZ
1542–91

Upon a Gloomy Night

Upon a gloomy night,
With all my cares to loving ardours flushed,
(O venture of delight!)
With nobody in sight
I went abroad when all my house was hushed.

In safety, in disguise,
In darkness up the secret stair I crept,
(O happy enterprise)
Concealed from other eyes
When all my house at length in silence slept.

Upon that lucky night
In secrecy, inscrutable to sight,
I went without discerning
And with no other light
Except for that which in my heart was burning.

It lit and led me through
More certain than the light of noonday clear
To where One waited near
Whose presence well I knew,
There where no other presence might appear.

Oh night that was my guide!
Oh darkness dearer than the morning's pride,
Oh night that joined the lover
To the beloved bride
Transfiguring them each into the other.

Within my flowering breast
Which only for himself entire I save
He sank into his rest
And all my gifts I gave
Lulled by the airs with which the cedars wave.

Over the ramparts fanned
While the fresh wind was fluttering his tresses,
With his serenest hand
My neck he wounded, and
Suspended every sense with its caresses.

Lost to myself I stayed
My face upon my lover having laid
From all endeavour ceasing:
And all my cares releasing
Threw them amongst the lilies there to fade.

With a Divine Intention

Without support, yet well supported,
Though in pitch-darkness, with no ray,
Entirely I am burned away.
My spirit is so freed from every
Created thing, that through the skies,
Above herself, she's lifted, flies,
And as in a most fragrant reverie,
Only on God her weight applies.
The thing which most my faith esteems
For this one fact will be reported—
Because my soul above me streams
Without support, yet well supported.

What though I languish in the shades
As through my mortal life I go,
Not over-heavy is my woe,
Since if no glow my gloom invades,
With a celestial life I glow.
The love of such a life, I say,
The more benightedly it darkens,

Turns more to that to which it hearkens,
Though in pitch-darkness, with no ray.

Since I knew Love, I have been taught
He can perform most wondrous labours.
Though good and bad in me are neighbours
He turns their difference to naught
Then both into Himself, so sweetly,
And with a flame so fine and fragrant
Which now I feel in me completely
Reduce my being, till no vagrant
Vestige of my own self can stay.
And wholly I am burned away.

Romance IV

'Let it be done, then,' said the Father,
'For Your love's surpassing worth.'
And the moment he pronounced it
Was the creation of the Earth.

For the bride He built a palace
Out of His knowledge vast and grand,
Which in two separate compartments,
One high, one low, He wisely planned.

The lower storey was of endless
Differences composed: the higher
He beautified with wondrous jewels,
Refulgent with supernal fire.

That the bride might know her Bridegroom
In the true glory of His power,
In the top part He set the angels
In shining hierarchy to tower.

But, tenant of the lower mansion
Our human nature was assigned
Because its human composition
Falls short of the angelic kind.

And though the Being in two places
He divided in this way,
He composed of both one body
To house the Bride, who thus did say:

That the love of one sole Bridegroom
Made them into one sole Bride.
Those of the upper part possessed Him
In deathless joy beatified:

Those underneath, in hope and yearning,
Born of the faith He brings to birth,
By telling them that surely, sometime,
His love will magnify their worth;

Each one living in the other;
Samely loved, clothed, fed, and shod.
She, absorbed in Him forever,
She will live the Life of God.

The fish that from the stream is lost
Derives some sort of consolation
That in his death he pays the cost
At least of death's annihilation.
To this dread life with which I'm crossed
What fell death can compare, since I,
The more I live, the more must die.

When thinking to relieve my pain
I in the sacraments behold You
It brings me greater grief again
That to myself I cannot fold You.
And that I cannot see you plain
Augments my sorrows, so that I
Am dying that I do not die.

If in the hope I should delight,
Oh Lord, of seeing You appear,
The thought that I might lose Your sight,
Doubles my sorrow and my fear.
Living as I do in such fright,
And yearning as I yearn, poor I
Must die because I do not die.

Oh rescue me from such a death
My God, and give me life, not fear;
Nor keep me bound and struggling here
Within the bonds of living breath.
Look how I long to see You near,
And how in such a plight I lie
Dying because I do not die!

I shall lament my death betimes,
And mourn my life, that it must be
Kept prisoner by sins and crimes
So long before I am set free:
Ah God, my God, when shall it be?
When I may say (and tell no lie)
I live because I've ceased to die?

Coplas about the soul which suffers with impatience to see God

I live without inhabiting
Myself—in such a wise that I
Am dying that I do not die.

Within myself I do not dwell
Since without God I cannot live.
Reft of myself, and God as well,
What serves this life (I cannot tell)
Except a thousand deaths to give?
Since waiting here for life I lie
And die because I do not die.

This life I live in vital strength
Is loss of life unless I win You:
And thus to die I shall continue
Until in You I live at length.
Listen (my God!) my life is in You
This life I do not want, for I
Am dying that I do not die.

Thus in your absence and your lack
How can I in myself abide
Nor suffer here a death more black
Than ever was by mortal died.
For pity of myself I've cried
Because in such a plight I lie
Dying because I do not die.

Verses written after an ecstasy of high exaltation

I entered in. I know not where,
And I remained, though knowing naught,
Transcending knowledge with my thought.

Of when I entered I know naught,
But when I saw that I was there
(Though where it was I did not care)
Strange things I learned, with greatness fraught.
Yet what I heard I'll not declare.
But there I stayed, though knowing naught,
Transcending knowledge with my thought.

Of peace and piety interwound
This perfect science had been wrought,
Within the solitude profound
A straight and narrow path it taught,
Such secret wisdom there I found
That there I stammered, saying naught,
But topped all knowledge with my thought.

So borne aloft, so drunken-reeling,
So rapt was I, so swept away,
Within the scope of sense or feeling
My sense or feeling could not stay.
And in my soul I felt, revealing,
A sense that, though its sense was naught,
Transcended knowledge with my thought.

The man who truly there has come
Of his own self must shed the guise;
Of all he knew before the sum
Seems far beneath that wondrous prize:
And in this lore he grows so wise
That he remains, though knowing naught,
Transcending knowledge with his thought.

The farther that I climbed the height
The less I seemed to understand
The cloud so tenebrous and grand
That there illuminates the night.
For he who understands that sight
Remains for aye, though knowing naught,
Transcending knowledge with his thought.

This wisdom without understanding
Is of so absolute a force
No wise man of whatever standing
Can ever stand against its course,
Unless they tap its wondrous source,
To know so much, though knowing naught,
They pass all knowledge with their thought.

This summit all so steeply towers
And is of excellence so high
No human faculties or powers
Can ever to the top come nigh.
Whoever with its steep could vie,
Though knowing nothing, would transcend
All thought, forever, without end.

If you would ask, what is its essence—
This summit of all sense and knowing:
It comes from the Divinest Presence—
The sudden sense of Him outflowing,
In His great clemency bestowing
The gift that leaves men knowing naught,
Yet passing knowledge with their thought.

LUIS DE GONGORA
1561–1627

From *The Spectre of the Rose*

Learn, flowers, from me, what parts we play
From dawn to dusk. Last noon the boast
And marvel of the fields, today
I am not even my own ghost.

The fresh aurora was my cot,
The night my coffin and my shroud;
I perished with no light, save what
The moon could lend me from a cloud.
And thus, all flowers must die—of whom
Not one of us can cheat the doom.

Learn, flowers, from me, etc.

What most consoles me for my fleetness
Is the carnation fresh with dew,
Since that which gave me one day's sweetness
To her conceded scarcely two:
Ephemerids in briefness vie
My scarlet and her crimson dye.

Learn, flowers, from me, etc.

The jasmine, fairest of the flowers,
Is least in size as in longevity.
She forms a star, yet lives less hours
Than it has rays. Her soul is brevity.
Could ambergris a flower be grown
It would be she, and she alone!

Learn, flowers, from me, etc.

The gillyflower, though plain and coarse,
Enjoys on earth a longer stay,
And sees more suns complete their course

As many as there shine in May.
Yet better far a marvel die
Than live a gillyflower, say I!

Learn, flowers, from me, etc.

To no flower blooming in our sphere did
The daystar grant a longer pardon
Than to the Sunflower, golden-bearded
Methusalem of every garden,
Eyeing him through as many days
As he shoots petals forth like rays.

Yet learn from me, what parts we play
From dawn to dusk. Last noon the boast
And marvel of the fields, today
I am not even my own ghost.

FRANCISCO DE QUEVEDO
1580–1645

On a Chaplain's Nose

Limblike to his own snout, projecting there,
A man was hung. Sufficient it appeared
For all the scribes and pharisees to share,
Protruding like a swordfish from his beard.
It seemed an ill-set dial-hand, a pensile
Alembic, or an elephant, whose hose
Is turned the wrong way up, and less prehensile.
Ovid's was far less noseyfied a nose.

It seems the beak and ram of some huge galley,
Or pyramid of Egypt. The Twelve Tribes
Of noses it exceeds and circumscribes.
For sheer nasality it has no tally.
A nose so fiercely nasal in its bias
Would even spoil the face of Ananias.

On Lisi's Golden Hair

When you shake loose your hair from all controlling,
Such thirst of beauty quickens my desire
Over its surge in red tornadoes rolling
My heart goes surfing on the waves of fire.
Leander, who for love the tempest dares,
It lets a sea of flames its life consume:
Icarus, from a sun whose rays are hairs,
Ignites its wings and glories in its doom.
Charring its hopes (whose deaths I mourn) it strives
Out of their ash to fan new phoenix-lives
That, dying of delight, new hopes embolden.
Miser, yet poor, the crime and fate it measures
Of Midas, starved and mocked with stacks of treasures,
Or Tantalus, with streams that shone as golden.

RUBÉN DARÍO
(Félix Rubén García-Sarmiento), Nicaraguan
1867–1916
After Rubén Dario

One day an earthquake seemed to pass
I felt, with sudden dread,
As if a Babel made of glass
Were splintering in my head.

With Pascal's travelling abyss
I've toured: with Baudelaire
Have felt the wing of madness hiss
And graze my standing hair.

I know the insect in the ointment,
The weevil in the bread,
The eternal ache of disappointment
To all achievement wed.

195

I whittled up my pens like sticks
And ribboned them with rhyme:
Like banderillas to transfix
The changing hump of time.

But one must win at any price
And fight, to the last breath,
To be the Conqueror of Vice,
Of Madness, and of Death.

FEDERICO GARCÍA LORCA
1899–1936

Preciosa and the Wind

Beating upon the moon of parchment
Preciosa with her tambourine
Comes down by an amphibious path
Of laurel shade and crystal sheen.
The silence bare of any star,
Scared by the jangled sound she rings,
Falls where the deep sound of the ocean
Starry with fish, resounds and sings.
Amongst the peaks of the sierra
Slumber the coast-guard carbineers
Keeping a watch upon the towers
Where English folk have lived for years.
Beating on her moon of parchment,
Preciosa comes with rhythmic fall;
To see her come the rude wind rises,
The wind that does not sleep at all.
A huge Saint Christopher stark naked
Full of celestial tongues of air,
He looks upon the girl, and plays
On a sweet pipe that isn't there.

'Allow me, girl, to lift your skirt
And let me see you plain and clear.
Open to my ancient fingers
The blue rose of your beauty, dear!'

Preciosa flings away her tambour,
And runs, and runs, and does not tire
And the Big-Man-Wind pursues her
With a burning sword of fire.
The sea has puckered up its rumour,
All pale as death the olives grow.
The shrill flutes of the shadows sing.
So does the smooth gong of the snow.

Preciosa run! or the green wind
Will surely have you by the hair!
Run, Preciosa! run like mad!
Look out! He nearly got you there!
The satyr of the setting stars
With all his glittering tongues of air.

Preciosa, terrified to death,
Runs into the first house she sees,
Where high above the lofty pines,
The English Consul lives at ease.

Alarmed to hear her piercing screams
Come rushing down three carbineers
With their black cloaks hugged tightly round them
And caps pulled down about their ears.

A tumbler full of lukewarm milk
The Englishman provides in haste
And a goblet full of gin
Which Preciosa will not taste.

And while she tells her story weeping
And they are listening, without pause
Against the roof-top tiles above them
The wind in fury gnashed his jaws.

Saint Michael

From the verandahs they are seen
Along the rocky mountain tracks—
Mules, and the shadows of the mules,
With loads of sunflowers on their backs.

197

His eyes amongst the shadows
Are tarnished with enormous night
And up the spirals of the air
Passes the dawn with salty light.

A sky of mules as white as milk
Closes its glazed, mercurial eyes
Imposing on the twilight hush
A period to hearts and sighs.
The water makes itself so cold
That nobody to touch it dares,
Mad water, running naked stark
Along the rocky mountain stairs.
Saint Michael, laden with his laces,
In the church-alcove where he camps
Is showing off his lordly thighs
Surrounded by a ring of lamps.

Archangel of domestic meekness,
When the stroke of midnight rings
He feigns a sweet fictitious anger
Of nightingales and rustling wings.
He sings amongst the stained glass windows,
Ephebus of three thousand eves
Fragrant with water of Cologne
But far away from flowers and leaves.

Waves on the shore compose a poem;
Each in its window-bay rejoices:
The river borders of the moon
Lose in reeds to gain in voices.
Flashy 'monolas' from the slums
Come chewing sunflower seeds and pips
With their occult, enormous bums
Like brazen planets in eclipse.
Tall gentlemen come down the way
With ladies sorrowful and frail
Wan with the thoughts of yesterday
And memories of the nightingale.

And the Bishop of Manila,
So poor and saffron-blinded, then
Says a Mass which has two edges
One for the women, one for men.

Saint Michael stayed content and quiet
Up in his garret in the tower
In his skirts, cascading finery,
Where crystals, lace and trinkets shower,
Saint Michael, ruler of the lamps,
And of the Offices and Paters,
Poised in the Berber eminence
Of crowds and wondering spectators.

Ballad of the Black Sorrow

O Soledad of all my sorrows,
Like a stampeding horse that raves
And when it meets the sea at last
Is swallowed outright by the waves!
'Do not remind me of the sea
That with the same black sorrow grieves
Over the country of the olives
Under the rumour of the leaves.'

In the fresh water of the larks
Refresh your body, and release
Your weary heart, O Soledad
Montoya! to repose in peace.

Away down there the river sings
The skirt-flounce of the sky and leaves.
Crowning itself with pumpkin flowers
The new light rustles through the sheaves.
O sorrow of the gipsy people,
Clean sorrow lonely as a star,
O sorrow of the hidden fountain
And of the daybreak seen afar!

Adam

The morning by a tree of blood was dewed
And near to it the newborn woman groans.
Her voice left glass within the wound, and strewed
The window with a diagram of bones.

Meanwhile the day had reached with steady light
The limits of the fable, which evades
The tumult of the bloodstream in its flight
Towards the dim cool apple in the shades.

Adam, within the fever of the clay,
Dreams a young child comes galloping his way,
Felt in his cheeks, with double pulse of blood.

But a dark other Adam dreaming yearned
For a stone neuter moon, where no seeds bud,
In which that child of glory will be burned.

Song of the Horseman

Córdoba.
Remote and lonely.

Jet-black mare and full round moon,
With olives in my saddle bags,
Although I know the road so well
I shall not get to Córdoba.

Across the plain, across the wind,
Jet-black mare and full red moon,
Death is gazing down upon me,
Down from the towers of Córdoba.

Ay! The road so dark and long.
Ay! My mare so tired yet brave.
Death is waiting for me there
Before I get to Córdoba.

Córdoba.
Remote and lonely.

Saint Gabriel

A lad as graceful as a reed
With shoulders broad and body slight,
With a skin of moonlit apples,
Sad mouth, and large eyes brimmed with light,
Like a nerve of burning silver
Round the deserted streets and square;
His shining shoes of patent leather
Trample the dahlias of the air
With their two rhythms that resound
Celestial dirges as they pace.
On all the seacoast is not found
A palm to equal him in grace,
Nor emperor that wears a crown,
Nor any wandering star in space.
When to his jasper breast he stoops
His forehead in that pensive way,
The night seeks out the lowliest plain
Because she wants to kneel and pray.
For the Archangel Gabriel
Lonely guitars sing on the breeze,
The tamer of the turtle-doves
And enemy of the willow-trees.
—Saint Gabriel, the child is weeping
Within his mother's womb alone.
Do not forget the suit of clothes
The gipsies gave you as your own.
Annunciation of the Kings,
So richly mooned, so poorly dressed,
Opens the door into the street
To entertain her starry guest.
The archangel Saint Gabriel,
Between a lily and a smile,
Great-grandson of the high Giralda,
Had been approaching all this while.
In the embroidery of his jacket
The crickets palpitate and sing
And all the stars that lit the night,
Turning to bells, began to ring.
'Saint Gabriel, you see me here

Pierced with three nails of fierce delight.
Your glory from my burning face
Suns forth the jasmines opening white.'
'God is with you, Annunciation,
Brown beauty of the gipsy kind,
You'll have a son more beautiful
Than rushes waving in the wind.'
'Saint Gabriel, dearer than my eyes,
Dear Gabriel of my days and hours!
To seat you here I visualize
A bank of sweet carnation flowers.'
'God is with you, Annunciation,
So richly mooned, so poorly dressed,
Your son will have a little mole
And three red gashes on his chest.'
'Saint Gabriel, how your glory shines!
Dear Gabriel of my life and veins!
Down in the bottom of my breasts
I feel the warm white milk that drains.'
'God is with you, Annunciation,
Mother of dynasties without end!
Your eyes burn like the barren plains
Through which the lonely horsemen wend.'
The baby sings within the breast
Annunciation to surprise.
Three seedlets of the almond green
Are trembling in his tiny cries.
Saint Gabriel through the silent air
Went up a ladder to the sky;
And all the stars of night were turned
To everlasting flowers on high.

Romance of the Civil Guard of Spain

Their horses are as black as night
Upon whose hoofs black horseshoes clink;
Upon their cloaks, with dismal sheen,
Shine smears of wax and ink.
The reason why they cannot weep
Is that their skulls are full of lead.

With souls of patent leather
Along the roads they tread.
Hunchbacked and nocturnal,
You feel when they're at hand
Silences of india-rubber
And fears like grains of sand.
They travel where they like,
Concealing in their skulls of neuters
A blurred astronomy of pistols
And shadowy six-shooters.

O city of the gipsy people!
Flags at the corners of the streets.
With calabashes and the moon
And cherries candied into sweets.
O city of the gipsy people!
Who can forget you who has seen?
City of sorrow and of musk
With towers of cinnamon between.
When the night-time has arrived,
The night-time of the night,
Gipsy folk upon their anvils
Are forging suns and darts of light.
A wounded horse arrives and runs
To all the doors with plaintive whine.
Cocks of glass are crowing loud
At Jerez of the Frontier-Line.
Around the corner of surprise
The wind burst naked on the sight,
In the night, the silver night-time,
In the night-time of the night.

The Virgin and Saint Joseph
Have left their castanets behind them
And come to ask the gipsies
If they will help to find them.
The Virgin like a Mayoress
Is sumptuously gowned
In silver chocolate paper
With almond necklets wound.
Saint Joseph moves his arms
In a silken cloak entwined
And with three Persian sultans

Pedro Domecq comes behind.
The crescent in the ecstasy
Of a white stork is dreaming
And over the flat roof-tops
Come flags and torches streaming.
Weeping before their mirrors
Hipless dancers mope and pine.
Water and shadow, shade and water
At Jerez of the Frontier-Line.

O city of the gipsies
With flags so fair to see,
Extinguish your green lamps, for here
Comes the Respectability!
O city of the gipsies
Who can forget you there?
Leave her distant from the sea
Without a comb to part her hair!

Two by two in double file
They reached the City of the Fair.
A sigh of everlasting flowers
Invades the cartridge-belts they wear.
A double nocturne of black cloth,
Their dark invasion naught deters.
Heaven to their approach appears
Merely a window-front of spurs.

The city multiplied its doors
Which, free from fear, had gaped asunder,
And through them forty Civil Guards
Enter to sack and plunder.
The clocks had stopped: the brandy
In bottles, with scared expedition,
Disguised itself with bleak November,
In order to avoid suspicion.
A flight of long-drawn screams
Ascended to the weathercock
While sabres cut the breeze with which
Their hoofs collide and shock.
The aged gipsy women fled
Along the twilight pavings,
Taking their drowsy horses

And pots filled with their savings.
Along the almost-upright streets
Sinister cloaks advance, all black
And leave a transitory vortex
Of whirling scissors in their track.

In the gateway of Bethlehem
The gipsies gather in a crowd.
Saint Joseph full of wounds,
Lays out a maiden in her shroud.
The sound of hard, sharp rifle-fire
Through all the darkness shocks and jars.
The Virgin cures the children
With the saliva of the stars.
But all the while the Civil Guard,
Advancing, sow the conflagration,
In which so tender, young and naked,
Is roasted the imagination.
Rosa of the Camborios
Groans in a door beside the way
With her two amputated breasts
Beside her on a tray.
The other girls rush round
Chased by their flying hair
While roses of black powder
Burst round them in the air.

When all the roofs in furrows
Across the soil were strown
The morning swayed its shoulders
In a vast profile of stone.

O city of the gipsies!
The Civil Guard retires at last
Along the tunnel of the silence,
While the flames are mounting fast.

O city of the gipsies, who
That saw you could forget you soon?
Let them seek you in my forehead
The playground of the sands and moon.

Sonnet—Tall silver ghost, the wind of midnight sighing

Tall silver ghost, the wind of midnight sighing
In pity opened up my ancient wound
With his grey hand: then went and left me lying
Where with my own sad longing I had swooned.

This wound will give me life: from it will come
Pure light and blood that issues without rest,
A rift wherein the nightingale, now dumb,
May find a grove, a sorrow, and a nest.

O what a gentle rumour stirs my brain!
Beside the simplest flower I'll lay my pain
Where floats, without a soul, your beauty's pride.

Then to a ruddy gold will change the vagrant
Stream, as my blood flows out into the fragrant
Dew-sprinkled thickets of the riverside.

FROM THE PORTUGUESE

PERO MEOGO
Mediaeval

Love Song—Tell me, my daughter,
my pretty young daughter

Tell me, my daughter, my pretty young daughter,
What kept you so long at the fountain for water?
(I've fallen in Love)

Tell me my daughter, my beautiful thing,
What caused you to linger beside the cold spring?
(I've fallen in Love)
I loitered, dear mother, so long by the fountain
For stags had been coming to drink from the mountain.
(I've fallen in Love)
I waited so long for the water to clear
Because it was churned into mud by the deer.
(I've fallen in Love)
You are lying, my girl, for your lover, I think:
Since I saw no stag coming down to the brink.
(I've fallen in Love)
You are lying, my daughter, for love it must be,
For I never saw stag which could trouble the Sea.

GIL VICENTE
c. 1470–1536
Rowing go the rowers

Rowing go the rowers
In a ship of great delight.
The captain at the helm

The Son of God is Light.
Angels at the oars
Rowed with all their might.
The flag of hope was flying
Lovely to the sight.
The mast was of endurance
Like crystal shining bright.
The sails were stitched with faith
And filled the world with light.
The seashore was serene
With not a wind in flight.

LUIZ VAZ DE CAMÕES
1524–80

The Sailor-Girl

Mother, my sighs unfurl
Forth on the seas to sally
With one in yonder galley
To be a sailor-girl.

O Mother mine, if only
I were where I would go!
I hate this Love so lonely,
This Love that loves him so,
This Cupid who's a churl,
This Babe who is my gaoler,
This longing for a sailor—
To be a sailor-girl!

He who all knots unravels
One he cannot unbind—
That though the spirit travels
The body stays behind.
With him for whom I'm dying
I'll go (or die—you'll see!)
All for a sailor trying
A sailor-girl to be.

What a despotic thing
The Tyrant Babe decreed
That One who is a King
For Love should have to bleed!
In such a wise, ah me!
Daily do I grow paler
For one who is a sailor
A sailor-girl to be.

Say, waves, if yet before
You ever saw so slender
A maiden, or so tender,
Go smiling from the shore!
From Babes that act the Demon
What mischiefs are not due?
To travel with my seaman
I'll be a sailor too!

Seven long years was Jacob herding sheep

Seven long years was Jacob herding sheep
For Laban, lovely Rachel's grim old father,
It was not for that mean old man, but rather
For her, he worked—the prize he longed to reap.
Days passed in expectation of one day.
That day of days became his sole idea.
But the old father swindled him with Leah
And gave him the wrong girl, with whom he lay.
The disillusioned shepherd, thus denied,
As if he'd never merited his bride,
Began another seven years' indenture.
Seven years more he laboured, staunch and strong,
Saying 'A longer contract I would venture—
But life's too short to serve a love so long.'

Canção IX

There is a mountain, sterile, stark and dry,
Useless, abandoned, hideous, bare and bald,
From whose cursed precincts nature shrinks appalled,
Where no beast ever sleeps, where no birds fly,
No river runs, nor bubbling sources spring,
Nor one green bough with pleasant sighs to sing.
In common speech the name they call it by
Is Felix (unfelicitously given!)
By Nature it was placed
Just where a strait has riven
The Arabian from the Abyssinian waste,
Where Berenice used to stand of yore,
In that part of the shore
Where the sun, having burnt it, hides once more;

Thence can be seen the Cape which ends the coast
Of Africa, which runs up from the south,
Called 'Aromatic' by as vain a boast
But something far less flowery in the mouth
Of the wild native in his savage tongue.
(Though fragrant once, perhaps, when time was young.)
There by the sea, whose high tide-swollen spate
Strives twice a day to burst that narrow strait,
To languish for a spell
It was my cursed fate,
There in that fierce inhospitable hell,
Where Life would fain desert itself to see
Its splintered bits, ah me!
Scattered about the world by land and sea.

Here was I stranded, passing dreary days,
Laborious evil, dolorous days and lonely,
Days full of toil, grief, rage, and long delays—
Not having for my adversaries only
Life, and the burning sun, and the chill tides,
With fierce, hot, roaring hurricanes besides,
But my own thoughts which only seemed my own
To play foul tricks on nature and deceive.
My memory too had grown

A thing to make me grieve,
Reviving some brief glories I had known
When in the world I sojourned, so to double,
By contrast, all my suffering and trouble,
By keeping me aware
That in the world were long hours free from care.

There did I live wasting both life and time
With these vain thoughts, which to a height immense
Reared me so steeply on their wings to climb
That so much steeper was my fall from thence,
Dashed downward from those castles in the air
To reach whose height I ever more despair.
Imagination here was turned to grief
In unexpected sobs to find relief
And sighs which rent the air.
My captive spirit there,
Wounded all over to the tender quick,
Crowded all round with sorrows dense and thick,
Unshielded lay beneath the hailing shot
Of my accursèd lot,
Inexorable, fierce, and hell-begot.

There was not anywhere the least relief,
Nor any hope whereon to lay my head
And snatch a little rest, however brief.
All things for harm and suffering seemed bred
Save that I could not die: for to have died
Would baulk my angry fate, and was denied.
My groans made calm the stormy waves that rolled,
Importuned by my voice, the winds grew cold
Worn out with my lament.
Only the heavens cruel,
The stars, and fate, so fierce in its intent,
Found their amusement in the oft-renewal
Of my sad torments, showing off their spite
My wretched self to smite,
Poor earthly thing, and such a tiny mite!

O that amongst these labours I might only
Know that for certain I shall once behold,
But for one hour, two eyes I knew of old:
That my lament, so desolate and lonely,

Might reach the ears of that angelic sprite
Within whose view I lived in such delight:
And that she, turning backward in her mind,
Might, thinking of the times we've left behind,
Recall each sweet mistake,
Quarrel, or torment kind
I sought and suffered only for her sake:
And thus, remembering such things, were she
To feel a pang for me
And her own stony-heartedness to see:

Only to know this thing would mean, for me,
Peace through the rest of life that yet remains.
With that I could console my dreary pains.
Ah, Lady, Lady! Wealthy you must be
Since even to imagine you sustains,
Far from all pleasures, what remains of me
When in my thoughts your effigy I see
All pain and weariness turn tail and flee.
Alone your memory arms
My soul with fearless might
Against ferocious death and mortal harms.
New hopes come rushing to me from your charms,
New hopes, with which my brow serenely bright
Confronts the woes I fight
Turning them into memories of delight.

Here with these memories I remain, and sue
Of every amorous zephyr of the air
From your part of the world, some news of you.
I ask the birds which seem to fly from there
If they have seen you, when, and what you do,
What day and hour it was, with whom, and where.
Thus my tired life from day to day improves:
I win new spirits; something in me moves
Which conquers toil and fate
To feel that once again
I may return to see you at some date,
To love, and serve, and with you to remain.
Say when the time will come that ends my pain!
But my desire, that nothing can abate,
Pitiless as before,
Has opened up my suffering wounds once more.

Thus live I. If they ask you, Song, why I
Have not yet chance to die,
Tell them that I am dying: That is why.

Dear gentle soul, who went so soon away

Dear gentle soul, who went so soon away
Departing from this life in discontent,
Repose in that far sky to which you went
While on this earth I linger in dismay.
In the ethereal seat where you must be,
If you consent to memories of our sphere,
Recall the love which, burning pure and clear,
So often in my eyes you used to see!
If then, in the incurable, long anguish
Of having lost you, as I pine and languish,
You see some merit—do this favour for me:
And to the God who cut your life short, pray
That he as early to your sight restore me
As from my own he swept you far away.

From *the Lusiads*, Book VIII

Enduring now of Neptune, now of Mars,
The most inhuman perils and the scars,
Like Canace, self-sentenced and undone,
A pen in one hand, and a sword in one:
Now for my penury abhorred, evaded,
And now in foreign doss-houses degraded:
No sooner with a hope acquired, than straight
The deeper dashed from where I stood elate:
Now, with my life escaping on my back,
That hung upon a thread so thin and slack,
To save it was a miracle, no less
Than were our King for heathen to confess.
And yet, O Nymphs, these miseries, though great,
Suffice not to appease my angry fate,
Since all I've sung of others' woes and curses

Must be the prize and guerdon of my verses,
Replacing all the joys for which I yearn—
Honours, repose, and laurels: which to spurn,
New travails I have never proved before
Must be invented, and a thousand more.

MANUEL BARBOSA DU BOCAGE
1765–1805
Sonnet
My being turns to smoke in the mad strife

My being turns to smoke in the mad strife
Of passions which have whirled me in their wake.
How miserably blind was I to take
This human span for almost-endless life.
What countless suns the boastful fancy forges
To gild this false existence as it flows,
But now my slave-like nature undergoes
The blasting havoc of a life of orgies.

Pleasures, my tyrant cronies, in confusion,
Hurling you to the gulf of disillusion,
My thirsty soul no longer can be pent.
Before my light fails, grant, my God! that I,
(One moment saving what in years I spent),
Who knew not how to live, learn how to die!

MANUEL BANDEIRA
1886– (Brazilian)
Counsel

The world is pitiless and lewdly jeers
All tragedy. Anticipate your loss.
Weep silently, in secret. Hide your tears,
So to become accustomed to your cross.

Alone grief can ennoble us. She only
Is grand and pure. Then learn to love her now—
To be your muse, when you are left and lonely,
And lay the last green laurels on your brow.

She will be sent from Heaven. The seraphic
Language she speaks in, you should learn, for she
Can talk no other in your daily traffic,

When you receive her to replace your bride.
Pray humbly, too, to God, that she may be
A constant, kind companion at your side.

INDEX OF TITLES

INDEX OF FIRST LINES

219